Safe use of work equipment

Provision and Use of Work Equipment Regulations 1998

APPROVED CODE OF P
AND GUIDANCE

L22

HSE BOOKS

Approved Code of Practice and guidance

This Code has been approved by the Health and Safety Commission, with
the consent of the Secretary of State. It gives practical advice on how to
comply with the law. If you follow the advice you will be doing enough to
comply with the law in respect of those specific matters on which the Code
gives advice. You may use alternative methods to those set out in the Code
in order to comply with the law.

However, the Code has special legal status. If you are prosecuted for breach
of health and safety law, and it is proved that you did not follow the relevant
provisions of the Code, you will need to show that you have complied with
the law in some other way or a court will find you at fault.

The Regulations and Approved Code of Practice (ACOP) are accompanied
by guidance which does not form part of the ACOP. Following the
guidance is not compulsory and you are free to take other action. But if you
do follow the guidance you will normally be doing enough to comply with
the law. Health and safety inspectors seek to secure compliance with the law
and may refer to this guidance as illustrating good practice.

For convenience, the text of the Regulations is set out in *italic* type, with the
ACOP in **bold** type and the accompanying guidance in normal type.

Contents

Note: Regulations 31-35 and Schedules 2 and 3 are not given in full in this publication as they relate to power presses.

Editorial note

Since this Approved Code of Practice and Guidance was written, regulations 10 and 11(2) have been amended by the Health and Safety (Miscellaneous Amendments) Regulations 2002.

Regulation 10 now reads:

(1) Every employer shall ensure that an item of work equipment conforms at all times with any essential requirements, other than requirements which, at the time of its being first supplied or put into service in any place in which these Regulations apply, did not apply to work equipment of its type.

(2) In this regulation "essential requirements", in relation to an item of work equipment, means requirements relating to the design and construction of work equipment of its type in any of the instruments listed in Schedule 1 (being instruments which give effect to Community directives concerning the safety of products).

Regulation 11(2) now reads:

(a) the provision of fixed guards enclosing every dangerous part or rotating stock-bar where and to the extent that it is practicable to do so, but where or to the extent that it is not, then

(b) the provision of other guards or protection devices where or to the extent that it is practicable to do so, but where or to the extent that it is not, then

(c) the provision of jigs, holders and push-sticks or similar protection appliances used in conjunction with the machinery where and to the extent that it is practicable to do so,

and the provision of such information, instruction, training and supervision as is necessary.

The text of the PUWER Approved Code of Practice and Guidance has not yet been reviewed following these changes. Some other regulations referred to in the text have been superseded and the 'References' section has been updated to include the most recent publications available.

Notice of Approval

By virtue of section 16(1) of the Health and Safety at Work etc Act 1974 (the 1974 Act), and with the consent of the Secretary of State for the Environment, Transport and the Regions pursuant to section 16(2) of the 1974 Act, the Health and Safety Commission has on 7 July 1998 approved the Code of Practice entitled *Safe use of work equipment*.

The Code of Practice comes into effect on 5 December 1998.

The Code of Practice gives practical guidance with respect to section 2 of the 1974 Act, the requirements of the Provision and Use of Work Equipment Regulations 1998, the Management of Health and Safety at Work Regulations 1992 (as amended by the Management of Health and Safety at Work (Amendment) Regulations 1994 and the Health and Safety (Young Persons) Regulations 1997) and the Workplace (Health, Safety and Welfare) Regulations 1992.

Signed

ROSEMARY BANNER
Secretary of the Health and Safety Commission

Dated this 5th day of October 1998.

Introduction

Introduction

This document on the Provision and Use of Work Equipment Regulations 1998 (PUWER 98) has been prepared by the Health and Safety Executive (HSE) for the Health and Safety Commission (HSC) after consultation with industry. These Regulations, which deal with providing and using work equipment, are set out in full along with the Approved Code of Practice and guidance material.

The Provision and Use of Work Equipment Regulations 1998

1   The Provision and Use of Work Equipment Regulations 1998 (PUWER 98) are made under the Health and Safety at Work etc Act 1974 (HSW Act) and come into force on 5 December 1998. PUWER 98 brings into effect the non-lifting aspects of the Amending Directive to the Use of Work Equipment Directive (AUWED). The primary objective of PUWER 98 is to ensure that work equipment should not result in health and safety risks, regardless of its age, condition or origin.

What does PUWER 98 apply to?

2   PUWER 98 applies to the provision and use of all work equipment, including mobile and lifting equipment.

Where does PUWER 98 apply?

3   It applies to all workplaces and work situations where the HSW Act applies and extends outside Great Britain to certain offshore activities in British territorial waters and on the UK Continental Shelf.

Who needs to read this?

4   Anyone with responsibility directly or indirectly for work equipment and its use, for example employers, employees, the self-employed and those who hire work equipment. Throughout this document we have referred to the employer and self-employed people who have duties as 'you'. Where the guidance is addressed to some other duty holder, for example a competent person, the text makes it clear who it is intended for.

What is in the document?

5   This document contains:

(a)   the PUWER 98 Regulations;

(b)   the Approved Code of Practice (ACOP); and

(c)   guidance material that has been written to help people use these Regulations.

HSE is publishing separate guidance specific to particular industry sectors. These link the requirements of PUWER 98 to the specialised work equipment used in industry sectors such as agriculture and construction.

What is an Approved Code of Practice (ACOP)?

6   The formal status of ACOP material is set out on page (ii) of this publication. ACOP material gives practical guidance on how to comply with the law. If you follow the advice in the ACOP you will be doing enough to ensure compliance with the law on the matters that it covers. ACOP material has special legal status. If you are prosecuted for a breach of health and safety law,

Guidance

1

and it is proved that you did not follow the relevant provisions of the ACOP, you will need to show that you have complied with the law in some other way or a court will find you at fault.

What is guidance?

7   Guidance material describes practical means of complying with the Regulations. It does not have special status in law, but is seen as best practice. Following the guidance is not compulsory and you are free to take other action. But if you do follow the guidance you will normally be doing enough to comply with the law. Health and safety inspectors seek to secure compliance with the law and may refer to this guidance as illustrating good practice.

Other HSC/E information

8   You should also take account of any relevant HSC/HSE publications giving guidance on other regulations, industries or equipment. There is a reference section at the back of this document. Up-to-date information on these publications can be obtained from HSE's Infoline which deals with public telephone requests (08701 545500).

Background

The Use of Work Equipment Directive and PUWER 92

9   PUWER 98 replaces PUWER 92 which implemented the first European Community (EC) Directive about work equipment, the Use of Work Equipment Directive (UWED). This required all Member States of the EC to have the same minimum requirements for the selection and use of work equipment.

The Amending Directive to the Use of Work Equipment Directive and PUWER 98

10   The European Council of Ministers agreed a further Directive about work equipment in 1995. This was the Amending Directive to the Use of Work Equipment Directive (AUWED). AUWED extended the requirements of UWED. PUWER 98 brought the requirements of AUWED into British law.

11   PUWER 98, while replacing PUWER 92, continues its requirements in addition to introducing the new measures required by AUWED. This was done to ensure that the law relating to work equipment was consolidated into one set of legislation.

AUWED's new requirements

12   AUWED's main new requirements concern mobile work equipment, lifting equipment and the inspection of work equipment. The 'hardware' requirements of AUWED outline physical features that relate to the equipment itself and the 'software' requirements consist of the management provisions. The specific requirements for mobile work equipment have been implemented through PUWER 98. The lifting requirements have been implemented through the Lifting Operations and Lifting Equipment Regulations 1998 (LOLER). The inspection requirements are incorporated in both PUWER 98 and LOLER.

Other changes - PUWER 92 to PUWER 98

13   PUWER 98 differs from PUWER 92 in a number of other ways. They are:

2

(a) an extension of the definition of 'work equipment' to include installations;

(b) an extension of the duty holder application to include a duty on people who have control of work equipment such as plant hire;

(c) guidance and ACOP material about regulation 7 (specific risks);

(d) changes to regulation 10 (conformity with Community requirements);

(e) minor changes to regulation 18 (control systems) as a result of a change required by AUWED;

(f) new regulations to replace the previous regulations dealing with power presses.

Lifting operations and lifting equipment

14   The lifting requirements of AUWED are brought into effect through a set of regulations called LOLER. LOLER replaces most of the existing legislation on lifting, for example lifting law that applies to factories, offices, shops, railway premises and construction sites. In doing so, it creates a single set of regulations that apply to all sectors.

15   Though PUWER 98 applies to all lifting equipment, LOLER applies over and above the general requirements of PUWER 98, in dealing with specific hazards/risks associated with lifting equipment and lifting operations.

16   LOLER, its supporting ACOP and guidance material are not included in this document. They are found in document L113.[1]

Power presses

17   PUWER 98 revokes the Power Presses Regulations 1965 and the Power Presses (Amendment) Regulations 1972 (the Power Presses Regulations). To ensure that safety levels for power presses are maintained, Part IV of PUWER 98 contains specific regulations applying to power presses. This part of PUWER 98 and its supporting ACOP and guidance material is available separately in L112.[2]

Woodworking

18   PUWER 98 revokes the remaining requirements of the Woodworking Machines Regulations 1974 which concern the training of operators, removal of material cut by circular sawing machines and requirements for machines with two-speed motors. The other requirements of the Woodworking Machines Regulations 1974 were revoked by PUWER 92. Because of the high accident rate and inherent risks associated with woodworking machines, a separate ACOP with supporting guidance material has been produced concerning the safeguarding of woodworking machines and the training of people who use them. The ACOP and guidance material relating to woodworking machines is published in L114.[3]

What does PUWER 98 require?

19   PUWER 98 sets out important health and safety requirements for the provision and safe use of work equipment. PUWER 98 is set out as follows:

(a) Regulations 1 to 3 deal with the date PUWER 98 comes into force, interpretation of the Regulations (definition of terms used in the Regulations), where PUWER 98 applies and who has duties under the Regulations.

(b) Regulations 4 to 10 are the 'management' duties of PUWER 98 covering selection of suitable equipment, maintenance, inspection, specific risks, information, instructions and training. It also covers the conformity of work equipment with legislation which brings into effect the requirements of EC Directives on product safety.

(c) Regulations 11 to 24 deal with the physical aspects of PUWER 98. They cover the guarding of dangerous parts of work equipment, the provision of appropriate stop and emergency stop controls, stability, suitable and sufficient lighting and suitable warning markings or devices.★

(d) Regulations 25 to 30 deal with certain risks from mobile work equipment.★

(e) Regulations 31 to 35 deal with the management requirements for the safe use of power presses.

(f) Regulations 36 to 39 cover transitional provisions, repeal of Acts and revocation of instruments.

(g) Schedule 1 lists the regulations implementing relevant EC 'product' Directives referred to in regulation 10.

(h) Schedule 2 lists the power presses to which regulations 32 to 35 do not apply.

(i) Schedule 3 lists the information to be contained in a report of a thorough examination of a power press, guard or protection device.

(j) Schedule 4 lists the regulations revoked by PUWER 98.

★ **Note:** Regulations 11-19 and 22-29 will not apply in certain circumstances - see regulation 10(2).

How PUWER 98 relates to other health and safety legislation

20   PUWER 1998 cannot be considered in isolation from other health and safety legislation. In particular, it needs to be considered with the requirements of the HSW Act.

21   Some of AUWED's provisions are not implemented by regulation in PUWER 98 as they are already covered adequately by the requirements of section 2 of the HSW Act. Supporting ACOP and guidance on these provisions is contained in this publication in paragraphs 31 to 54.

22   There is also some overlap between PUWER 98 and other sets of regulations, for example the Workplace (Health, Safety and Welfare) Regulations 1992 (workplace risks to pedestrians from vehicles) and the Health and Safety (Display Screen Equipment) Regulations 1992 (for example, on lighting) and the Personal Protective Equipment at Work Regulations 1992 (for example, on maintenance), the Construction (Health, Safety and Welfare) Regulations 1996 (for example, on standards for work equipment such as scaffolding) and the Road Vehicles (Construction and Use) Regulations 1986. If you comply with the more specific regulations, it will normally be sufficient to comply with the more general requirements in PUWER 98.

23   The Management of Health and Safety at Work Regulations 1992 (the Management Regulations) also have important general provisions relating to the safety of work equipment, including the requirement to carry out a risk assessment. This is discussed in the following paragraphs.

Risk assessment

24   Because of the general risk assessment requirements in the Management Regulations, there is no specific regulation requiring a risk assessment in PUWER. HSE has produced guidance in a booklet called *5 steps to risk assessment*.[4]

25   Risks to health and safety should be assessed taking into account matters such as the type of work equipment, substances and electrical or mechanical hazards to which people may be exposed.

26   Action to eliminate/control any risk might include, for example, during maintenance:

(a)   disconnecting the power supply to the work equipment;

(b)   supporting parts of the work equipment which could fall;

(c)   securing mobile work equipment so that it cannot move;

(d)   removing or isolating flammable or hazardous substances; and

(e)   depressurising pressurised equipment.

27   Other matters to consider include environmental conditions such as:

(a)   lighting;

(b)   problems caused by weather conditions;

(c)   other work being carried out which may affect the operation; or

(d)   the activities of people who are not at work.

How does PUWER 98 affect older health and safety legislation about work equipment?

28   PUWER 98 repeals or revokes most of the remaining legislation about work equipment. This is listed at regulations 38 and 39 (referring to Schedule 4) of PUWER 98.

Structure of the ACOP

29   This publication has ACOP material for PUWER 98. Regulations that have been carried forward unchanged from PUWER 92 do not have any ACOP material except for regulations 4, 7 and 9, where it is necessary to bring into effect AUWED (regulations 4 and 9) or where needed to clarify the meaning of a regulation (regulation 7). We have also included some ACOP and guidance material on aspects of the HSW Act, where relevant.

Links with other legislation and other health and safety principles

30   The requirements of ACOP and guidance material which follows link with

other health and safety legislation, for example the Workplace Regulations. These aspects are described, where relevant, in the following guidance. You may need to obtain further information on specific points and there is a list of useful references at the end of this publication.

The Health and Safety at Work etc Act 1974, Section 2

Introduction

31   AUWED contains some requirements for the management of work equipment. These requirements are fulfilled through Section 2 of the HSW Act and the new ACOP to support it which is reproduced in the following paragraphs.

The Health and Safety at Work etc Act 1974

Section 2.   (1)   It shall be the duty of every employer to ensure, so far as is reasonably practicable, the health, safety and welfare at work of all his employees.

(2)   Without prejudice to the generality of an employer's duty under the preceding subsection, the matters to which that duty extends include in particular:

(a)   the provision and maintenance of plant and systems of work that are, so far as is reasonably practicable, safe and without risks to health;

(b)   arrangements for ensuring, so far as is reasonably practicable, safety and absence of risks to health in connection with the use, handling, storage and transport of articles and substances;

(c)   the provision of such information, instruction, training and supervision as is necessary to ensure, so far as is reasonably practicable, the health and safety at work of his employees;

(d)   so far as is reasonably practicable as regards any place of work under the employer's control, the maintenance of it in a condition that is safe and without risks to health and the provision and maintenance of means of access and egress from it that are safe and without risks;

(e)   the provision and maintenance of a working environment for his employees that is, so far as is reasonably practicable, safe, without risks to health, and adequate as regards facilities and arrangements for their welfare at work.

Erecting or dismantling work equipment

32   You should ensure that work equipment is erected or dismantled in a safe way, in particular observing any manufacturers' or suppliers' instructions where they exist.[a]

(a)   This implements point 1.2 of Annex II of AUWED: 'Work equipment must be erected or dismantled under safe conditions, in particular observing any instructions which may have been furnished by the manufacturer.'

33   The assembly and dismantling of some items of work equipment, for example airbridges at airports, may be subject to the requirements of the Construction (Design and Management) Regulations 1994.

Systems of work

34   Work equipment should be erected, assembled or dismantled safely and without risk to health. Safe systems of work and safe working practice should be

followed to achieve this. A safe system of work is a formal procedure which should be followed to ensure that work is carried out safely and is necessary where risks cannot be adequately controlled by other means.

35   The work should be planned and potential hazards identified. You should ensure that the systems of work to be followed are properly implemented and monitored and that details have been communicated to those at risk.

36   HSE's leaflet *Managing health and safety: Five steps to success*[5] gives further detailed information about safe systems of work.

Competence of workers

37   The knowledge, experience and abilities of the people carrying out the work should be considered. They should be competent to carry out the work safely.

Groups at risk

38   You have a duty under health and safety law to ensure, as far as is reasonably practicable, the health, safety and welfare of your employees. When carrying out an assessment of the risk to their health and safety, you should identify groups of workers that might be particularly at risk such as young or disabled people. The outcome of your risk assessment will be helpful in meeting your duty to provide information, instruction, training and supervision necessary to ensure the health and safety of your employees. You will want to take account of factors such as their competence, experience, maturity, etc. Formal qualifications, training certificates, aptitude tests, etc might be used to help identify competence.

Mobile work equipment and the HSW Act

39   Sections 2(1) and 2(2) of the HSW Act cover the risks to pedestrians from the movement of mobile work equipment.

Risks from self-propelled work equipment

40   This section of ACOP and guidance deals with some of the risks from the movement of mobile work equipment. This includes risks of pedestrians being struck by vehicles, or their loads.

Assessing risks from self-propelled work equipment

41   The Management Regulations require you to carry out a risk assessment. Ths risk assessment will identify the hazards, help you evaluate the risks and also decide how to control the risks. Appropriate preventive and protective measures should be taken in the light of the risks identified. The risks which the use of mobile work equipment can create where pedestrians are present include the danger of people being struck, crushed or run over by self-propelled work equipment or being struck by an object falling from a vehicle.

Dealing with the risks from self-propelled mobile equipment

42   The precautions covered here that may be required to control the risks which the use of self-propelled work equipment can create for pedestrians are:

(a)   separation of pedestrians and self-propelled mobile work equipment;

7

(b)   traffic rules;

(c)   traffic signs;

(d)   planning traffic routes;

(e)   traffic speed.

43   Regulation 17 of the Workplace Regulations and its supporting ACOP material also deal with the organisation, etc of traffic routes and the organisation of workplaces so that pedestrians and vehicles can circulate in a safe manner. This requirement should be considered together with this publication to achieve compliance with both PUWER 98 and the Workplace Regulations.

44   The explanations describing mobile work equipment are in Part III of PUWER 98.

Risks to pedestrians

45   You should take measures, where appropriate, to prevent pedestrians coming within the area of operation of self-propelled work equipment. Where this is not reasonably practicable, appropriate measures should be taken to reduce the risks involved, including the operation of appropriate traffic rules.(b)(c)(d)

(b)   *This implements point 2.2 of Annex II of AUWED: 'If work equipment is moving around in a work area, appropriate traffic rules must be drawn up and followed.'*

(c)   *This implements point 2.3 of Annex II of AUWED: 'Organisational measures must be taken to prevent workers on foot coming within the area of operation of self-propelled work equipment.' If work can be done properly, only if workers on foot are present, appropriate measures should be taken to prevent them from being injured by the equipment.'*

(d)   *This implements point 2.4 of Annex II of AUWED: ' The transport of workers on mechanically driven mobile work equipment is authorised only where safe facilities are provided to this effect. If work needs to be carried out during the journey, speeds must be adjusted as necessary.'*

46   Wherever possible you should keep pedestrians away from self-propelled work equipment. Where this is not possible you are required, so far as is reasonably practicable, to provide and maintain a safe system of work.

Traffic rules

47   Appropriate traffic rules should limit the risks to pedestrians and operators when mobile work equipment is in use, for example, fork-lift trucks operating in a loading bay where there are pedestrians and other vehicles. Traffic rules should be established as part of a safe system of work (see paragraph 35) following risk assessment.

Further guidance

48   Workplace transport safety is covered in detail in *Workplace transport safety.*[6] It covers the following topics:

(a)   accidents - numbers, costs and causes;

(b)   legal duties;

(c)   managing risks;

(d)   risk assessment;

(e)   organising for safety including control, communication, co-operation and competence;

(f)   a safe workplace;

(g)   vehicle safety;

(h)   maintenance;

(i)   selection and training of drivers and other employees;

(j)   contractors, visiting drivers and shared workplaces;

(k)   safe working practices;

(l)   reversing of vehicles;

(m)   parking of vehicles;

(n)   access onto vehicles;

(o)   loading and unloading;

(p)   tipping of loads;

(q)   sheeting and unsheeting of loads.

Lightning

49   AUWED requires that where work equipment may be struck by lightning while being used it must be protected as appropriate against the effects of the lightning. This requirement is implemented through the following ACOP and guidance material.

50   **You should ensure that, where there is a risk to workers arising from lightning strikes to work equipment when it is being used, appropriate safety precautions are followed.**[e]

(e)   This implements point 1.3 of Annex II of AUWED: 'Work equipment which may be struck by lightning whilst being used must be protected by devices or appropriate means against the effects of lightning.'

Assessing the risks from lightning

51   When assessing whether lightning protection is required for work equipment, you should consider whether:

(a)   the area is one in which lightning generally occurs;

(b)   the work equipment is tall or isolated;

(c)   the work equipment contains flammable or explosive substances;

(d)   large numbers of people will be affected by a lightning strike.

52   Types of work equipment which you should consider include:

(a)   cranes being used in isolated areas;

(b)   fairground equipment operating in similar conditions or in the open where large numbers of people are likely to be affected by a lightning strike;

(c)   employees engaged in field work - surveyors etc, where there is a possible risk of lightning strike if the surveying staff/prism is used during a lightning strike.

Lightning protection

53   Protection from lightning can be provided by conductors or insulation. There are circumstances where the best way of reducing the risk is to cease working during a lightning storm. For example, a golf professional should avoid playing or teaching during a storm as a metal golf club is an excellent conductor of lightning and golf is often played in open areas or near trees where lightning strikes are likely to occur. Likewise a surveying team may need to stop work during a storm as would certain utility workers.

Other information about lightning and lightning protection

54   Detailed information about lightning, risk assessment, the likelihood of lightning strike and suitable protection is contained in BS 6651:1999, the British Standard Code of Practice for protection of structures against lightning.

THE PROVISION AND USE OF WORK EQUIPMENT REGULATIONS 1998

PART I: INTRODUCTION

Regulation 1

PUWER 98
Regulation 1

PUWER 98

Citation and commencement

These Regulations may be cited as the Provision and Use of Work Equipment Regulations 1998 and shall come into force on 5th December 1998.

When does PUWER 98 come into force?

55   PUWER 98 comes into force on 5 December 1998. Some of the Regulations dealing with mobile work equipment do not come into effect until 5 December 2002. The date the Regulations will apply will depend on whether the work equipment is new, existing, or second-hand on 5 December 1998. These transitional arrangements can be found in regulation 37.

New work equipment

56   Items of work equipment first provided for use from 5 December 1998 (NEW WORK EQUIPMENT) will need to meet ALL the requirements of PUWER 98 (see paragraphs on regulation 10).

Existing work equipment

57   If work equipment is first provided for use before 5 December 1998 (EXISTING WORK EQUIPMENT), PUWER 98 regulations 1-24 and 31-39 come into force on 5 December 1998. These Regulations are essentially the same as the requirements of PUWER 92, except for regulation 6 and those relating to power presses. Regulations 26-30 which for existing mobile work equipment come into force from December 2002 form Part III of PUWER 98 and cover mobile work equipment. However, Parts I and II of PUWER 98 will apply to ALL mobile work equipment from 5 December 1998.

Second-hand work equipment

58   When existing work equipment is sold by one company to another and brought into use by the purchasing company from 5 December 1998, it becomes new work equipment in the sense of paragraph 56 even though it is second-hand. This means that the purchasing company will need to ensure that the work equipment meets the provisions of PUWER 98 before it is put into use.

'Provided for use'

59   The phrase 'provided for use' refers to the date on which work equipment is first supplied in the premises or undertaking. This is not the same as first brought into use. Provided for use does not necessarily mean that it has actually been put into use. For example, equipment delivered to a company before 5 December 1998 and put into storage would be considered to be 'existing equipment' even though it might remain in store and not be put into use until after that date. This is set out in regulation 37 which deals with the transitional provisions for these Regulations.

Guidance 1

Regulation 2   Interpretation

(1)   In these Regulations, unless the context otherwise requires -

"the 1974 Act" means the Health and Safety at Work etc. Act 1974;

"employer" except in regulation 3(2) and (3) includes a person to whom the requirements imposed by these Regulations apply by virtue of regulation 3(3)(a) and (b);

"essential requirements" means requirements described in regulation 10(1);

"the Executive" means the Health and Safety Executive;

"inspection" in relation to an inspection under paragraph (1) or (2) of regulation 6 -

(a)   means such visual or more rigorous inspection by a competent person as is appropriate for the purpose described in the paragraph;

(b)   where it is appropriate to carry out testing for the purpose, includes testing the nature and extent of which are appropriate for the purpose;

"power press" means a press or press brake for the working of metal by means of tools, or for die proving, which is power driven and which embodies a flywheel and clutch;

"thorough examination" in relation to a thorough examination under paragraph (1), (2), (3) or (4) of regulation 32 -

(a)   means a thorough examination by a competent person;

(b)   includes testing the nature and extent of which are appropriate for the purpose described in the paragraph;

"use" in relation to work equipment means any activity involving work equipment and includes starting, stopping, programming, setting, transporting, repairing, modifying, maintaining, servicing and cleaning;

"work equipment" means any machinery, appliance, apparatus, tool or installation for use at work (whether exclusively or not);

and related expressions shall be construed accordingly.

(2)   Any reference in regulations 32 to 34 or Schedule 3 to a guard or protection device is a reference to a guard or protection device provided for the tools of a power press.

(3)   Any reference in regulation 32 or 33 to a guard or protection device being on a power press shall, in the case of a guard or protection device designed to operate while adjacent to a power press, be construed as a reference to its being adjacent to it.

(4)   Any reference in these Regulations to -

(a)   a numbered regulation or Schedule is a reference to the regulation or Schedule in these Regulations so numbered; and

(b)   a numbered paragraph is a reference to the paragraph so numbered in the regulation in which the reference appears.

Inspection

60   The term 'inspection' is used in PUWER 98. The purpose of the inspection is to identify whether the equipment can be operated, adjusted and maintained safely and that any deterioration (for example, defect, damage, wear) can be detected and remedied before it results in unacceptable risks.

Use

61   The definition of 'use' is wide and includes all activities involving work equipment such as stopping or starting the equipment, repair, modification, maintenance and servicing. In addition to operations normally considered as use, cleaning and transport of the equipment are also included. In this context 'transport' means, for example, using a lift truck to carry goods around a warehouse.

Work equipment

62   The scope of 'work equipment' is extremely wide. It covers almost any equipment used at work, including:

(a)   'tool box tools' such as hammers, knives, handsaws, meat cleavers etc;

(b)   single machines such as drilling machines, circular saws, photocopiers, combine harvesters, dumper trucks, etc;

(c)   apparatus such as laboratory apparatus (Bunsen burners etc);

(d)   lifting equipment such as hoists, lift trucks, elevating work platforms, lifting slings, etc;

(e)   other equipment such as ladders, pressure water cleaners etc;

(f)   an installation such as a series of machines connected together for example a paper-making line or enclosure for providing sound insulation or scaffolding or similar access equipment (except where the Construction (Health, Safety and Welfare) Regulations 1996 impose more detailed requirements).

63   'Installation' does not include an offshore installation but would include any equipment attached or connected to it. The word 'installation' has replaced the phrase used in PUWER 92 'any assembly of components which in order to achieve a common end are arranged and controlled so that they function as a whole'.

64   The following are not classified as work equipment:

(a)   livestock;

(b)   substances (for example, acids, alkalis, slurry, cement, water);

(c)   structural items (for example, walls, stairs, roof, fences);

(d)   private car.

Motor vehicles

65   Motor vehicles which are not privately owned fall within the scope of PUWER 98. However, the more specific road traffic legislation will take

precedence when these vehicles are used on public roads or in a public place. When such vehicles are used off the public highway and the road traffic law does not apply, for example on a dock road, PUWER 98 and the HSW Act would normally take precedence unless relevant local by-laws are in operation - for example, road traffic by-laws at some airports. Car drivers should hold a Department of Transport driving licence and cars should be maintained to the normal standards required for use on the public highway, ie they should have an MOT certificate, where necessary, or maintained to equivalent standard where statutory testing is not a legal requirement.

Aircraft

66   The design, operation and maintenance of aircraft airworthiness is subject to other specific legislation, such as the Air Navigation (No 2) Order 1995 and Civil Aviation Authority (CAA) standards, such as JAR25 'Design requirements for large aeroplanes' which is an annex to EC Regulation 3922/91. This legislation takes precedence over PUWER 98.

'For use at work'

67   The phrase 'for use at work' has also been added to the end of the definition of 'work equipment'. Section 52(1)(b) and (c) of the HSW Act define this as 'an employee is at work throughout the time when he is in the course of his employment, but not otherwise and a self-employed person is at work throughout such time as he devotes to work as a self-employed person.'

Regulation 3

Application

(1)   *These Regulations shall apply -*

(a)   *in Great Britain; and*

(b)   *outside Great Britain as sections 1 to 59 and 80 to 82 of the 1974 Act apply by virtue of the Health and Safety at Work etc. Act 1974 (Application outside Great Britain) Order 1995 [g] ("the 1995 Order").*

(2)   *The requirements imposed by these Regulations on an employer in respect of work equipment shall apply to such equipment provided for use or used by an employee of his at work.*

(3)   *The requirements imposed by these Regulations on an employer shall also apply -*

(a)   *to a self-employed person, in respect of work equipment he uses at work;*

(b)   *subject to paragraph (5), to a person who has control to any extent of -*

(i)   *work equipment;*

(ii)   *a person at work who uses or supervises or manages the use of work equipment; or*

(iii)   *the way in which work equipment is used at work,*

and to the extent of his control.

(g) *SI 1995/263.*

14

(4)   Any reference in paragraph (3)(b) to a person having control is a reference to a person having control in connection with the carrying on by him of a trade, business or other undertaking (whether for profit or not).

(5)   The requirements imposed by these Regulations shall not apply to a person in respect of work equipment supplied by him by way of sale, agreement for sale or hire-purchase agreement.

(6)   Subject to paragraphs (7) to (10), these Regulations shall not impose any obligation in relation to a ship's work equipment (whether that equipment is used on or off the ship).

(7)   Where merchant shipping requirements are applicable to a ship's work equipment, paragraph (6) shall relieve the shore employer of his obligations under these Regulations in respect of that equipment only where he has taken all reasonable steps to satisfy himself that the merchant shipping requirements are being complied with in respect of that equipment.

(8)   In a case where the merchant shipping requirements are not applicable to the ship's work equipment by reason only that for the time being there is no master, crew or watchman on the ship, those requirements shall nevertheless be treated for the purpose of paragraph (7) as if they were applicable.

(9)   Where the ship's work equipment is used in a specified operation paragraph (6) shall not apply to regulations 7 to 9, 11 to 13, 20 to 22 and 30 (each as applied by regulation 3).

(10)   Paragraph (6) does not apply to a ship's work equipment provided for use or used in an activity (whether carried on in or outside Great Britain) specified in the 1995 Order save that it does apply to -

(a)   the loading, unloading, fuelling or provisioning of the ship; or

(b)   the construction, reconstruction, finishing, refitting, repair, maintenance, cleaning or breaking up of the ship.

(11)   In this regulation -

"master" has the meaning assigned to it by section 313(1) of the Merchant Shipping Act 1995; [h]

"merchant shipping requirements" means the requirements of regulations 3 and 4 of the Merchant Shipping (Guarding of Machinery and Safety of Electrical Equipment) Regulations 1988 [i] *and regulations 5 to 10 of the Merchant Shipping (Hatches and Lifting Plant) Regulations 1988* [j]*;*

"ship" has the meaning assigned to it by section 313(1) of the Merchant Shipping Act 1995 save that it does not include an offshore installation;

"shore employer" means an employer of persons (other than the master and crew of any ship) who are engaged in a specified operation;

"specified operation" means an operation in which the ship's work equipment is used -

(a)   by persons other than the master and crew; or

(b)   where persons other than the master and crew are liable to be exposed to a risk to their health or safety from its use.

(h)   1995 c.21.
(i)   SI 1988/1636, amended by SI 1988/2274.
(j)   SI 1988/1639, amended by SI 1988/2274.

Where PUWER 98 applies

68   PUWER 98 applies:

(a)   to all work equipment used where the HSW Act applies, ie to all sectors, not only factories, offices and shops but also, for example schools, universities, hospitals, hotels, places of entertainment and offshore oil and gas installations;

(b)   to work equipment used in the common parts of shared buildings (such as lifts), private roads and paths on industrial estates and business parks and temporary work sites, including construction sites;

(c)   throughout Great Britain and has effect wherever work is done by the employed or the self-employed except for domestic work in a private household;

(d)   to homeworkers and will also apply to hotels, nursing homes and similar establishments and to parts of workplaces where 'domestic' staff are employed such as the kitchens of hostels or sheltered accommodation.

Application offshore

69   PUWER applies offshore as the HSW Act applies by virtue of the Health and Safety at Work etc Act 1974 (Application outside Great Britain) Order 1995 (SI 1995/263). This Order applies the Act to offshore installations, wells, pipelines and pipeline works, and to connected activities within the territorial waters of Great Britain or in designated areas of the United Kingdom Continental Shelf, plus certain other activities within territorial waters.

How does PUWER apply to marine activities?

70   Ships are subject to merchant shipping legislation which is dealt with by the Maritime and Coastguard Agency. Apart from certain regulations and in certain circumstances, PUWER 98 does not apply to ships' work equipment, no matter where it is used. However, regulations 7-9, 11-13, 20-22 and 30 of PUWER 98 will apply in what are called 'specified operations'. Specified operations are where the ships' equipment is used by those other than the master and crew of the vessel or where only the master and crew are involved in the work, but other people are put at risk by the work being carried out.

71   Where shore-based workers are to use ship's equipment, and their employers wish to take advantage of this disapplication from PUWER 98, they are required by the Regulations to take reasonable steps to satisfy themselves that the appropriate merchant shipping requirements have been met. The ship's records should normally contain sufficient information to satisfy reasonable enquiries.

72   PUWER 98 may apply to other work equipment not belonging to but used on board a ship, for example where a shore-based contractor carries out work on a ship within territorial waters. Work equipment used in such circumstances would be subject to PUWER 98 but PUWER 98 does not apply to foreign registered vessels on passage.

73   Most mobile offshore installations are also ships. PUWER will apply without qualification to mobile installations while at or near their working stations and when in transit to their working stations. PUWER will also apply without qualification to work equipment used on ships for the purposes of carrying out activities in connection with offshore installations or wells and for pipeline works.

Who has duties under PUWER 98?

74   PUWER 98 places duties on:

(a)   employers;

(b)   the self-employed; and

(c)   people who have control of work equipment.

The duty on people who have control of work equipment reflects the way that work equipment is used in industry where there may not necessarily be a direct 'employment' relationship between the user and the person who controls the work equipment. For example, where a subcontractor carries out work at another person's premises with work equipment provided by that person or someone else who controls the equipment but not its use, such as a plant hire company. This approach is in line with that taken in the Construction (Health, Safety and Welfare) Regulations 1996 and in LOLER.

Who does not have duties under PUWER 98?

75   If you provide work equipment as part of a work activity for use by members of the public, you do not have duties under PUWER 98. Examples are compressed air equipment on a garage forecourt or lifts provided for use by the public in a shopping mall. In such circumstances members of the public will continue to be protected by the requirements of the HSW Act, principally sections 3 and 4.

What do you need to do if you have duties under PUWER 98?

76   If you have duties under PUWER 98 you need to ensure that work equipment you provide for use at work complies with PUWER 98.

Employer's duties

77   If you are an employer (whether as an individual, partnership or company) you have a duty to ensure that items of work equipment provided for your employees and the self-employed working for you comply with PUWER 98.

Self-employed people's duties

78   If you are self-employed you have a duty to ensure that work equipment you provide for work or use at work complies with PUWER 98.

The duties of 'those in control of work equipment'

79   If you provide work equipment for use at work where you do not control its use or the premises where it is to be used, you should still ensure that the work equipment complies with PUWER 98. People in control of non-domestic premises who provide work equipment which is used by other people at work should also comply with PUWER 98. PUWER places duties on employers and the self-employed; offshore this includes owners, operators and contractors. Their duties cover both their own employees and, as people having control of work equipment, other workers who may be affected. Meeting these duties where a number of employers and their employees are involved requires co-operation and co-ordination of activities. For example, the owner of a multi-occupied building has a legal responsibility to ensure that a lift complies with the Regulations, and the main contractor of a construction site would be responsible for a scaffold.

17

Where employees provide their own work equipment for use at work

80   PUWER 98 also covers situations where employers allow their employees to provide their own work equipment. For example, where builders use their own trowels or hammers.

Employees' duties

81   If you are an employee you do not have any specific duties under PUWER 98. These are covered in other legislation, in particular in section 7 of the HSW Act and regulation 12 of the Management Regulations.

The Trade Union Reform and Employment Rights Act 1993

82   This Act implements the employment protection requirements of the EC Health and Safety Framework Directive. The Act applies to all employees including those working offshore. It gives rights to all employees, regardless of their length of service, hours of work or age. The Act entitles employees to complain to an industrial tribunal about dismissal, selection for redundancy or any other matter for taking or proposing to take specified types of action on health and safety grounds, such as leaving the workplace in circumstances of danger or taking appropriate steps to protect themselves or others from the danger.

Multi-occupancy or multi-occupier sites

83   On multi-occupancy or multi-contractor sites where several duty holders may share the use of equipment, you can agree amongst yourselves that one of you takes responsibility for ensuring that the equipment complies with PUWER 98 (and any other relevant legislation), particularly regulation 9 of the Management Regulations. The following paragraphs examine such situations in detail in the construction and offshore sectors. Similar principles apply in other sectors.

Application to the construction industry

84   In the construction industry items of work equipment on sites are often used by a number of different contractors. Regulation 3 places a duty on each contractor to ensure that any work equipment used by their employees (or themselves in the case of self-employed contractors) conforms to, and is used in accordance with, these Regulations.

85   It also requires, to the extent that their control allows, the same duty from those who exercise control over the equipment or the way that it is used. For example, those hiring out equipment for others to use will often play the leading role in inspecting and maintaining the equipment since they determine the maintenance schedules and availability of their machines. On the other hand, the users may be more directly concerned, for example, with organising, instructing and training their employees to use it safely since the conduct of their own employees is clearly a matter for them rather than the hirer.

86   The actions of others such as hirers may assist employers and the self-employed to meet their duties. However, that does not reduce the employer's or the self-employed's duty to ensure their own compliance with the Regulations. Effective co-ordination between the parties involved can be essential in order to satisfy their own legal duties.

87   The arrangements required by regulation 9 of the Management Regulations have been strengthened by the Construction (Design and Management) Regulations 1994 (CDM).

88   The CDM Regulations require the appointment of a single person or firm ('the principal contractor') to co-ordinate health and safety matters on site. The principal contractor also has a duty to ensure that all contractors co-operate on health and safety matters. Where the use of equipment by a wide range of personnel from a number of different employers requires particular attention or co-ordination, this should be addressed in the construction phase health and safety plan. Co-operation and exchanging information is vital when equipment is shared. All users need to know:

(a)   who is responsible for the co-ordination of the equipment;

(b)   that changes in conditions of use need to be reported to that person;

(c)   whether there are any limitations on the use of the equipment; and

(d)   how the equipment can be used safely.

Application to the offshore industry

89   PUWER places duties on employers and the self-employed; offshore this includes owners, operators and contractors. Their duties cover both their own employees and, as people having control of work equipment, other workers who may be affected. Meeting these duties where a number of employers and their employees are involved requires co-operation and co-ordination of activities. The person in control of an operation should ensure that adequate arrangements are in place to ensure that work equipment provided for use at work is suitable, properly used and maintained, etc. This will often be an installation owner or operator, for example, but contractors who take equipment offshore are primarily responsible for risks arising from that equipment.

90   Legal requirements for co-operation between offshore duty holders are set out in the Offshore Installations (Safety Case) Regulations 1992 and the Offshore Installations and Pipeline Works (Management and Administration) Regulations 1995.

91   Equipment for use on offshore installations that is safety-critical, as defined by regulation 2(1) of the Offshore Installations (Safety Case) Regulations 1992, will be subject to the verification arrangements required elsewhere in those Regulations.

PART II: GENERAL

Suitability of work equipment

(1)   Every employer shall ensure that work equipment is so constructed or adapted as to be suitable for the purpose for which it is used or provided.

(2)   In selecting work equipment, every employer shall have regard to the working conditions and to the risks to the health and safety of persons which exist in the premises or undertaking in which that work equipment is to be used and any additional risk posed by the use of that work equipment.

How risk assessment and the Management Regulations link with PUWER 98

92   This regulation deals with the safety of work equipment from three aspects:

(a)   its initial integrity;

(b)   the place where it will be used; and

(c)   the purpose for which it will be used.

93   The selection of suitable work equipment for particular tasks and processes makes it possible to reduce or eliminate many risks to the health and safety of people at the workplace. This applies both to the normal use of the equipment as well as to other operations such as maintenance.

94   The risk assessment carried out under regulation 3(1) of the Management Regulations will help to select work equipment and assess its suitability for particular tasks.

95   Most dutyholders will be capable of making the risk assessment themselves using expertise within their own organisations to identify the measures which need to be taken regarding their work equipment. In a few cases, for example where there are complex hazards or equipment, it may need to be done in conjunction with the help of external health and safety advisers, appointed under regulation 6 of the Management Regulations.

96   For many items of work equipment, particularly machinery, you will know from experience what measures need to be taken to comply with previous legal requirements. Generally, these measures will ensure compliance with PUWER 98. Where this is not the case, there is usually a straightforward method of identifying the measures that need to be taken, because these are described in either general guidance or guidance specific to a particular industry or piece of equipment. However, the user will need to decide whether these are appropriate.

97   Where guidance does not exist, or is not appropriate, the main factors that need to be taken into account are the severity of any likely injury or ill health likely to result from any hazard present, the likelihood of that happening and the numbers of people exposed. You can then identify the measures that need to be taken to eliminate or reduce the risk to an acceptable level.

98   Further guidance on risk assessment is to be found in the ACOP on the Management Regulations (see paragraph 24) which includes advice on the selection of preventive and protective measures and HSE's free leaflet entitled *5 steps to risk assessment*.[4]

Ergonomics

99   One of the factors to be considered is ergonomics.

100   **When selecting work equipment, employers should take account of ergonomic risks.**

101   Ergonomic design takes account of the size and shape of the human body and should ensure that the design is compatible with human dimensions. Operating positions, working heights, reach distances, etc can be adapted to accommodate the intended operator. Operation of the equipment should not

place undue strain on the user. Operators should not be expected to exert undue force or stretch or reach beyond their normal strength or physical reach limitations to carry out tasks. This is particularly important for highly repetitive work such as working on supermarket checkouts or high speed 'pick and place' operations.

102   Risks could arise as a result of using mobile work equipment, for which the measures in Part III are relevant. However, for existing equipment (that which was in use before 5 December 1998) the requirements in Part III do not come into force until 5 December 2002. Therefore, until this date, you do not need to comply with Part III when considering the selection of suitable mobile work equipment. However, where the risks are significant, you may wish to select alternative equipment anyway.

Regulation 4(1)

103   Equipment must be suitable, by design, construction or adaptation, for the actual work it is provided to do. This means in practice that when you provide work equipment you should ensure that it is suitable for the work to be undertaken and that it is used in accordance with the manufacturer's specifications and instructions. If work equipment is adapted it must still be suitable for its intended purpose.

104   This requirement provides the focal point for the other Regulations - for example, compliance with regulation 10 should ensure the initial integrity of equipment in many cases, and compliance as appropriate with the specific requirements of regulations 11 to 24.

Regulation 4(2)

105   This requires you to assess the location in which the work equipment is to be used and to take account of any risks that may arise from the particular circumstances. Such factors can invalidate the use of work equipment in a particular place. For example, electrically powered equipment is not suitable for use in wet or flammable atmospheres unless it is designed for this purpose. In such circumstances you should consider selecting suitably protected electrical equipment or alternative pneumatically or hydraulically powered equipment.

106   **You should ensure that work equipment is installed, located and used in such a way as to reduce risks to users of work equipment and for other workers, such as ensuring that there is sufficient space between the moving parts of work equipment and fixed or moving parts in its environment.**[k]

107   **When determining the suitability of work equipment, you should ensure that where appropriate:**

(a)   **all forms of energy used or produced; and**

(b)   **all substances used or produced**

can be supplied and/or removed in a safe manner.[k]

(k)   *This implements point 1.1 of Annex II of AUWED: 'Work equipment must be installed, located and used in such a way as to reduce risks to users of the work equipment and for other workers, for example by ensuring that there is sufficient space between the moving parts of work equipment and fixed or moving parts in its environment and that all forms of energy and substances used or produced can be supplied and/or removed in a safe manner.'*

108   You should ensure that where mobile work equipment with a combustion engine is in use there is sufficient air of good quality.[(l)]

(l)   This implements point 2.5 of Annex II of AUWED: 'Mobile work equipment with a combustion engine may not be used in working areas unless sufficient quantities of air presenting no health or safety risk to workers can be guaranteed.'

109   You should also take account of the fact that work equipment itself can sometimes cause risks to health and safety in particular locations which would otherwise be safe. Such an example is a petrol engine generator discharging exhaust fumes into an enclosed space.

Why ventilation may be necessary

110   Exhaust gases from mobile work equipment with a combustion engine may contribute significantly to airborne pollution in workplaces. For example, in motor vehicle workshops, underground car parks, in buildings where fork-lift trucks are used and in tunnels. In such circumstances a high standard of ventilation and/or extraction may be necessary to allow the combustion process to take place and to dilute toxic combustion products (such as carbon monoxide, carbon dioxide and oxides of nitrogen) to an acceptable level. Combustion products can be harmful to health if there is insufficient fresh air for people to breathe.

When to ventilate workplaces

111   Ventilation requirements will vary depending on the type of fuel, condition of the engine and pattern of use. If mobile work equipment is fitted with pollution control services, lower ventilation rates may be necessary. The method of ventilation will depend on where the work equipment is used, for example in a warehouse or a tunnel and if sufficient air of good quality is not naturally available it may need to be supplied.

How to ensure there is sufficient clean air

112   Examples of how to ensure there is sufficient clean air include:

(a)   the exhausts of stationary vehicles under test or repair should be connected to exhaust removal systems;

(b)   flexible exhaust systems or box filters should be used where necessary;

(c)   natural and/or mechanical ventilation should be used where necessary;

(d)   air quality should be monitored on a regular basis to ensure that the control systems in place are working adequately.

Ventilation requirements of the Workplace (Health, Safety and Welfare) Regulations 1992 (the Workplace Regulations)

113   Regulation 6 of the Workplace Regulations and its supporting ACOP contain general requirements about ventilation of the workplace and equipment used to ventilate workplaces.

The Confined Spaces Regulations 1997

114   The ACOP to the Confined Spaces Regulations 1997 does not allow the use of petrol-fuelled internal combustion engines in a confined space unless

22

special precautions are taken. A confined space is one which is substantially or entirely closed and there will be a reasonably foreseeable risk of serious injury from hazardous substances or conditions within the space or nearby. Other forms of fuel such as diesel or gas are nearly as dangerous and are inappropriate unless adequate precautions are taken. Where their use is unavoidable, adequate ventilation needs to be provided to prevent a build-up of harmful gases, for example from leakage of the fuel or the exhaust system and to allow the engine to operate properly.

115   The exhaust from engines must be vented to a safe place well away from the confined space and downwind of any ventilator intakes for the confined space. You should check for the build-up of harmful gases within the confined space. Fuelling of portable engine-driven equipment should be conducted outside the confined space except in rare cases such as tunnelling. Using such equipment within the confined space requires constant atmospheric monitoring for gas. Full guidance and ACOP material on the Confined Spaces Regulations 1997 is contained in HSE's publication *Safe work in confined spaces*.[7]

Control of Substances Hazardous to Health Regulations 1999 (COSHH)

116   Regulation 7 of COSHH requires employers to prevent or control the exposure of employees to substances hazardous to health. ACOP material on the COSHH Regulations is contained in HSE's *COSHH ACOP*.[8]

Regulation 4

Suitability of work equipment

(3)   Every employer shall ensure that work equipment is used only for operations for which, and under conditions for which, it is suitable.

(4)   In this regulation "suitable" means suitable in any respect which it is reasonably foreseeable will affect the health or safety of any person.

Regulation 4(3)

117   This requirement concerns each particular process for which the work equipment is to be used and the conditions under which it will be used. You must ensure that the equipment is suitable for the process and conditions of use. Examples include:

(a)   a circular saw is generally not suitable for cutting a rebate whereas a spindle moulding machine would be suitable because it can be guarded to a high standard;

(b)   knives with unprotected blades are often used for cutting operations where scissors or other cutting tools could be used, reducing both the probability and severity of injury.

Regulation 5

Maintenance

(1)   Every employer shall ensure that work equipment is maintained in an efficient state, in efficient working order and in good repair.

(2)   Every employer shall ensure that where any machinery has a maintenance log, the log is kept up to date.

Application of the regulation

118   This regulation builds on the general duty in the HSW Act, which requires work equipment to be maintained so that it is safe. It does not cover the maintenance process (that is covered by the general duties of the HSW Act) or the construction of work equipment so that maintenance can be carried out without risk to health or safety (these are the subject of regulation 10 and regulation 22).

119   It is important that equipment is maintained so that its performance does not deteriorate to the extent that it puts people at risk. In regulation 5, 'efficient' relates to how the condition of the equipment might affect health and safety. It is not concerned with productivity. Some parts of equipment such as guards, ventilation equipment, emergency shutdown systems and pressure relief devices have to be maintained to do their job at all times. The need to maintain other parts may not be as obvious, for example failure to lubricate bearings or replace clogged filters might lead to danger because of seized parts or overheating. Some maintenance routines affect both the way the equipment works and its safety. Checking and replacing worn or damaged friction linings in the clutch on a guillotine will ensure it operates correctly, but could also prevent the drive mechanism jamming, so reducing the risk of repeat uncovenanted strokes.

Frequency of maintenance

120   Equipment may need to be checked frequently to ensure that safety-related features are functioning correctly. A fault which affects production is normally apparent within a short time; however, a fault in a safety-critical system could remain undetected unless appropriate safety checks are included in maintenance activities.

121   The frequency at which maintenance activities are carried out should also take into account the:

(a)   intensity of use - frequency and maximum working limits;

(b)   operating environment, for example marine, outdoors;

(c)   variety of operations - is the equipment performing the same task all the time or does this change?

(d)   risk to health and safety from malfunction or failure.

Maintenance management

122   The extent and complexity of maintenance can vary substantially from simple checks on basic equipment to integrated programmes for complex plant. In all circumstances, for maintenance to be effective it needs to be targeted at the parts of work equipment where failure or deterioration could lead to health and safety risks. Maintenance should address those parts which have failed or are likely to deteriorate and lead to health and safety risks.

123   A number of maintenance management techniques could be used:

(a)   planned preventive;

(b)   condition-based;

(c)   breakdown.

APPROPRIATE TECHNIQUES SHOULD BE SELECTED THROUGH RISK ASSESSMENT AND USED INDEPENDENTLY OR IN COMBINATION TO ADDRESS THE RISKS INVOLVED.

124 Simple hand tools usually require minimal maintenance, but could require repair or replacement at intervals. More complex powered equipment will normally be accompanied by a manufacturer's maintenance manual, which specifies routine and special maintenance procedures to be carried out at particular intervals. Some of the procedures will be necessary to keep the equipment in working order, others will be required for safety reasons.

125 It should be remembered that different maintenance management techniques have different benefits.

(a) Planned preventive maintenance involves replacing parts and consumables or making necessary adjustments at preset intervals so that risks do not occur as a result of the deterioration or failure of the equipment.

(b) Condition-based maintenance involves monitoring the condition of safety-critical parts and carrying out maintenance whenever necessary to avoid hazards which could otherwise occur.

(c) Breakdown maintenance involves carrying out maintenance only after faults or failures have occurred. It is appropriate only if the failure does not present an immediate risk and can be corrected before risk occurs, for example through effective fault reporting and maintenance schemes.

126 Where safety-critical parts could fail and cause the equipment, guards or other protection devices to fail and lead to immediate or hidden potential risks, a formal system of planned preventative or condition-based maintenance is likely to be needed.

127 Some equipment may not be owned by the user. Many items of plant and equipment are hired. It is important for both the hire company and the person responsible for hiring equipment to establish which party will carry out safety-related maintenance. This is particularly important for equipment on long-term hire and the terms of the agreement set out or recorded in writing.

128 In many cases, safety-related maintenance work is not carried out by the person with ultimate responsibility for the work equipment, in the mistaken belief that the other party will do it. If the hire company is some distance from the user site, it would be uneconomical for their staff to carry out simple checks and make minor adjustments, so the user may agree to carry them out. However, both parties should agree exactly what they are responsible for.

Maintenance log

129 There is no requirement for you to keep a maintenance log. However, it is recommended that you keep a record of maintenance for high-risk equipment. A detailed maintenance log can provide information for future planning of maintenance activities and inform maintenance personnel and others of previous action taken.

130 If you have a maintenance log, you should keep it up to date.

131 Maintenance procedures should be carried out in accordance with any manufacturer's recommendations which relate to the equipment, for example periodic lubrication, replacement and adjustment of parts.

PUWER 98

Guidance 5

132 However, additional maintenance measures may be required if particularly arduous conditions of use are foreseen or have been experienced in use. There may be times when these additional measures need to be reviewed and revised in the light of ongoing operating experiences.

Maintenance workers

133 Maintenance work should only be done by those who are competent to do the work. For details of the information, instructions and training required, see also regulations 8 and 9.

Regulation 6

PUWER 98

Regulation 6

Inspection

(1)   Every employer shall ensure that, where the safety of work equipment depends on the installation conditions, it is inspected -

(a)   after installation and before being put into service for the first time; or

(b)   after assembly at a new site or in a new location,

to ensure that it has been installed correctly and is safe to operate.

(2)   Every employer shall ensure that work equipment exposed to conditions causing deterioration which is liable to result in dangerous situations is inspected -

(a)   at suitable intervals; and

(b)   each time that exceptional circumstances which are liable to jeopardise the safety of the work equipment have occurred,

to ensure that health and safety conditions are maintained and that any deterioration can be detected and remedied in good time.

PUWER 98

Guidance 6

Inspection

134 This requirement for the inspection of work equipment builds on the current but often informal practice of regular in-house inspection of work equipment, some of which is already recommended in other HSE guidance.

135 Inspection does not normally include the checks that are a part of the maintenance activity although certain aspects may well be common. Nor, for the purposes of this regulation, does inspection include a pre-use check that an operator may make before using the work equipment. Additionally, while inspections need to be recorded, such checks do not.

Identifying what needs to be inspected

ACOP

Regulation 6

136 **Where the risk assessment under regulation 3 of the Management of Health and Safety at Work Regulations 1992 has identified a significant risk to the operator or other workers from the installation or use of the work equipment, a suitable inspection should be carried out.**

PUWER 98

Guidance 6

Significant risk

137 A significant risk is one which could foreseeably result in a major injury or worse.

26

138 Inspection is only necessary where there is a significant risk resulting from:

(a) incorrect installation or re-installation;

(b) deterioration; or

(c) as a result of exceptional circumstances which could affect the safe operation of the work equipment.

139 The types of major injury are listed in Schedule 1 of the Reporting of Injuries, Diseases and Dangerous Occurrences Regulations 1995. They are reproduced in Appendix 1 of this publication.

Purpose of an inspection

140 The purpose of an inspection is to identify whether the equipment can be operated, adjusted and maintained safely and that any deterioration (for example defect, damage, wear) can be detected and remedied before it results in unacceptable risks.

What should be included in the inspection

141 **The extent of the inspection required will depend on the potential risks from the work equipment. Inspection should include, where appropriate, visual checks, functional checks and testing.**

142 The extent of the inspection that is needed will depend upon:

(a) the type of equipment;

(b) where it is used; and

(c) how it is used.

143 An inspection will vary from a simple visual external inspection to a detailed comprehensive inspection, which may include some dismantling and/or testing.

144 An inspection should always include those safety-related parts which are necessary for safe operation of equipment, for example overload warning devices and limit switches.

145 The level of inspection required would normally be less detailed and less intrusive than the thorough examination required for the purposes of regulation 33 on power presses and regulation 9 of LOLER for certain items of lifting equipment.

146 Some work equipment will need examinations and thorough examinations under other legislation such as the Pressure Systems Regulations, COSHH, Control of Lead at Work Regulations (CLAW), Control of Asbestos at Work Regulations (CAW). Inspections will only be needed for such work equipment if these other examinations do not fully cover all the significant health and safety risks which are likely to arise from the use of the equipment, in a way that satisfies the requirements of PUWER.

Testing

147 As part of an inspection, a functional or other test may be necessary to check that the safety-related parts, for example interlocks, protection devices,

controls, etc are working as they should be and that the work equipment and relevant parts are structurally sound, for example non-destructive testing of safety-critical parts. The need for any testing (for example non-destructive testing of safety-critical parts) should be decided by the competent person who determines the nature of the inspection.

Competent persons

148 You should ensure that persons who determine the nature of the inspections required and who carry out inspections are competent to do so.

149 The competent person should have the necessary knowledge and experience.

150 *'Determining the nature of the inspection'* - the knowledge and experience required by a person to determine the nature of the inspection needs to be sufficient for them to be able to decide what the inspection should include, how it should be done and when it should be carried out. Experienced, in-house employees such as a department manager or supervisor may be able to do this. They should know what will need to be inspected to detect damage or faults resulting from deterioration. They should also be able to determine whether any tests are needed during the inspection to see if the equipment is working safely or is structurally sound.

151 *'Carrying out the inspection'* - the person who actually carries out the inspection may not necessarily be the same person who determines the nature of the inspections. The actual inspection will normally be done by an in-house employee with an adequate knowledge of the equipment to:

(a) enable them to know what to look at (know the key components);

(b) know what to look for (fault-finding); and

(c) know what to do (reporting faults, making a record, who to report to).

Where necessary, you should give them appropriate information, instruction and training so they can carry out the inspection properly and avoid danger. They should also be aware of and able to avoid danger to themselves and others.

152 The necessary level of competence will vary according to the type of equipment and where and how it is used. For some equipment, the level of competence to determine the nature of the inspections or even to carry them out may not be available in-house, in which case the help of another body with relevant competence may be necessary. An example of this will be the person who carries out the annual inspection under these Regulations of some fairground rides.

Installation

153 Where work equipment is of a type where the safe operation is critically dependent on it being properly installed (or re-installed), and where failure to carry this out would lead to a significant risk to the operator, or other worker, you should arrange for a suitable inspection to be carried out before it is put into service.

154 Re-installation includes assembling the equipment at a new site or in a new location. Equipment that has been installed or re-installed is normally in a permanent or long-term location and is usually fixed in position. Installation or re-installation does not normally include re-positioning or moving equipment, particularly where there is no element of dismantling, re-assembling and/or fixing the equipment in position, or if its location is transitory. Examples of work equipment where safety is critically dependent on the installation conditions include those where guarding is provided by presence-sensing devices (such as light curtains used for paper-cutting guillotines or pressure sensitive mats used with tube-bending machines). These devices allow free access to the danger zone but should be positioned so that if anyone approaches the danger zone they will be detected and the hazardous functions stopped before injury can occur.

'Conditions causing deterioration' and 'Dangerous situations'

155 **Where work equipment is of a type where the safe operation is critically dependent on its condition in use and deterioration would lead to a significant risk to the operator or other worker, you should arrange for suitable inspections to be carried out.**

Equipment that should receive an inspection

156 The types of equipment whose use could result in significant risk as a result of deterioration and which may therefore need to be inspected include:

(a)   most fairground equipment;

(b)   machines where there is a need to approach the danger zone during normal operation such as horizontal injection moulding machines, paper-cutting guillotines, die-casting machines, shell-moulding machines;

(c)   complex automated equipment;

(d)   integrated production lines.

Equipment for which an inspection is not required

157 If failure or fault of the equipment cannot lead to significant risk or if safety is guaranteed through appropriate maintenance regimes (under regulation 5), inspection may not be necessary. Equipment unlikely to need an inspection includes office furniture, hand tools, non-powered machinery and also powered machinery such as a reciprocating fixed blade metal cutting saw.

Frequency of inspection

158 **The frequency of inspections should be based on how quickly the work equipment or parts of it are likely to deteriorate and therefore give rise to a significant risk. This should take into account the type of equipment, how it is used and the conditions to which it is exposed.**

159 The inspection frequency may be different for the same type of equipment because the rate of deterioration can vary in different situations. Where equipment is subject to frequent use in a harsh outdoor environment (for

example, at a coastal site or on a construction site), it is likely to need more frequent inspection than if it is used occasionally in an indoor environment such as a warehouse.

160   To ensure that appropriate inspection intervals and procedures are in place, they should be reviewed in the light of experience. Intervals between inspections can be lengthened if an inspection history has shown that deterioration is negligible or the interval between inspections should be shortened if substantial amounts of deterioration are detected at each inspection.

Exceptional circumstances

161   Regulation 6(2) states that an inspection is necessary 'each time that exceptional circumstances which are liable to jeopardise the safety of the work equipment have occurred.'

162   Exceptional circumstances which may result in the need for inspection include:

(a)   major modifications, refurbishment or major repair work;

(b)   known or suspected serious damage;

(c)   substantial change in the nature of use, for example from an extended period of inactivity.

Regulation 6

(3)   Every employer shall ensure that the result of an inspection made under this regulation is recorded and kept until the next inspection under this regulation is recorded.

Records

163   Records do not have to be kept in a particular form. They can be handwritten or stored electronically - from a pre-printed form to an entry in a diary. There are no legal requirements stating what they contain. However, a record should normally include:

(a)   information on the type and model of equipment;

(b)   any identification mark or number that it has;

(c)   its normal location;

(d)   the date that the inspection was carried out;

(e)   who carried out the inspection;

(f)   any faults; and/or

(g)   any action taken;

(h)   to whom the faults have been reported;

(i)   the date when repairs or other necessary action were carried out.

Regulation 6

(4)   Every employer shall ensure that no work equipment -

(a)   leaves his undertaking; or

(b)   if obtained from the undertaking of another person, is used in his undertaking, unless it is accompanied by physical evidence that the last inspection required to be carried out under this regulation has been carried out.

164   **The physical evidence should be appropriate to the type of work equipment being inspected.**

165   For large items of equipment for which inspection is necessary, the physical evidence can be in the form of a copy of the record of the last inspection carried out. For smaller items of equipment, a tagging, colour coding or labelling system can be used. The purpose of the physical evidence is to enable a user to check if an inspection has been carried out and whether or not it is current, where required, and also to determine the results of that inspection, by being able to link back from the physical evidence to the records.

Regulation 6

(5)   This regulation does not apply to -

(a)   a power press to which regulations 32 to 35 apply;

(b)   a guard or protection device for the tools of such power press;

(c)   work equipment for lifting loads including persons;

(d)   winding apparatus to which the Mines (Shafts and Winding) Regulations 1993 [(m)] apply;

(e)   work equipment required to be inspected by regulation 29 of the Construction (Health, Safety and Welfare) Regulations 1996 [(n)].

(m) SI 1993/302.
(n)   SI 1996/1592.

166   These inspection requirements do not cover the following work equipment as set out in regulation 6(5):

(a)   POWER PRESSES COVERED BY REGULATIONS 31-39 OF PUWER. These include mechanically driven presses or press brakes (called 'power press(es)' in this booklet) which are power driven, have a flywheel and clutch, and which are wholly or partly used to work metal. A clutch, in relation to a power press, is a device to impart the movement of the flywheel to any tool when required.

(b)   WORK EQUIPMENT FOR LIFTING LOADS INCLUDING PEOPLE. This is defined as work equipment for lifting or lowering loads and includes its attachments used for anchoring, fixing or supporting it. A load does include a person.

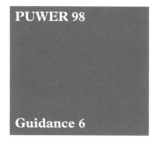
(c) Under the Mines (Shafts and Winding) Regulations 1993, WINDING APPARATUS means 'mechanically operated apparatus for lowering and raising loads through a (mine) shaft and includes a conveyance or counterweight attached to such apparatus and all ancillary apparatus.'

(d) Work equipment required to be inspected by regulation 29 of the Construction (Health, Safety and Welfare) Regulations 1996, such as SCAFFOLDING and EXCAVATION SUPPORTS.

Regulation 7

Specific risks

(1)   Where the use of work equipment is likely to involve a specific risk to health or safety, every employer shall ensure that -

(a)   the use of that work equipment is restricted to those persons given the task of using it; and

(b)   repairs, modifications, maintenance or servicing of that work equipment is restricted to those persons who have been specifically designated to perform operations of that description (whether or not also authorised to perform other operations).

(2)   The employer shall ensure that the persons designated for the purposes of sub-paragraph (b) of paragraph (1) have received adequate training related to any operations in respect of which they have been so designated.

167 You should ensure that, wherever possible, risks are always controlled by (in the order given):

(a) eliminating the risks, or if that is not possible;

(b) taking 'hardware' (physical) measures to control the risks such as the provision of guards; but if the risks cannot be adequately controlled;

(c) taking appropriate 'software' measures to deal with the residual (remaining) risk, such as following safe systems of work and the provision of information, instruction and training.

Normal operation

168 Where the risks from the use of work equipment cannot be adequately controlled by hardware measures, such as guards or protection devices, during its normal operation, it is particularly important that only the persons whose task it is should be allowed to use such equipment. They should have received sufficient information, instruction and training to enable them to carry out the work safely.

Repairs, modifications etc

169 Where the risks from the use of work equipment cannot be adequately controlled by hardware measures such as guards or protection devices during repair, maintenance, or other similar work, only persons who have received sufficient information, instruction and training to enable them to carry out the work safely should do the work. They shall be the designated person for the purpose of this regulation.

170 Specific risks can be common to a particular class of work equipment, for example the risks from a platen printing machine or from a drop forging machine. There can also be a specific risk associated with the way a particular item of work equipment is repaired, set or adjusted as well as with the way it is used.

171 The person whose normal work includes the use of a piece of work equipment will have been given 'the task of using it' and the instruction and training provided should be appropriate to that work. For someone using a grinding machine for example, training should cover the proper methods of dressing the abrasive wheels. For someone carrying out a turning operation on a lathe, the training should cover the devices which should be used if working with emery cloth to obtain the required finish on a workpiece.

172 The designated person to carry out repairs, etc will be the person whose work includes these activities. This person could be the operator of the equipment, provided that they have received relevant instruction and training. For example, the training for a person who has to change the knives on guillotines should include any devices which could be used, such as knife handles, as well as the system of work.

Regulation 8

Information and instructions

(1)   Every employer shall ensure that all persons who use work equipment have available to them adequate health and safety information and, where appropriate, written instructions pertaining to the use of the work equipment.

(2)   Every employer shall ensure that any of his employees who supervises or manages the use of work equipment has available to him adequate health and safety information and, where appropriate, written instructions pertaining to the use of the work equipment.

(3)   Without prejudice to the generality of paragraphs (1) or (2), the information and instructions required by either of those paragraphs shall include information and, where appropriate, written instructions on -

(a)   the conditions in which and the methods by which the work equipment may be used;

(b)   foreseeable abnormal situations and the action to be taken if such a situation were to occur; and

(c)   any conclusions to be drawn from experience in using the work equipment.

(4)   Information and instructions required by this regulation shall be readily comprehensible to those concerned.

How regulation 8 links with other health and safety law

173 This Regulation builds on the general duty in the HSW Act to provide employees with the information and instructions that are necessary to ensure, so far as is reasonably practicable, their health and safety. It also links with the general requirement in the Management Regulations to provide information to employees relating to their health and safety. The Health and Safety (Consultation with Employees) Regulations 1996 (HSCER) require employers to consult their employees on the information required under other regulations,

including PUWER 98, about risks to their health and safety and preventative measures in place.

What does regulation 8 require?

174   Regulation 8 places a duty on employers to make available all relevant health and safety information and, where appropriate, written instructions on the use of work equipment to their workforce. Workers should have easy access to such information and instructions and be able to understand them.

Written instructions

175   Regulation 8 refers to written instructions. This can include the information provided by manufacturers or suppliers of work equipment such as instruction sheets or manuals, instruction placards, warning labels and training manuals. It can also include in-house instructions and instructions from training courses. There are duties on manufacturers and suppliers to provide sufficient information, including drawings, to enable the correct installation, safe operation and maintenance of the work equipment. You should ask or check that they are provided.

Consultation with employees

176   Under the Consultation with Employees Regulations, employers must consult their employees about these matters before decisions and changes are made. HSE's booklet *A guide to the health and Safety (Consultation with Employees) Regulations 1996*[9] contains the HSCER Regulations and supporting guidance.

177   There are requirements for consultation within the Safety Representatives and Safety Committees Regulations 1977 which provide for the appointment of safety representatives by recognised trade unions. The Health and Safety (Consultation with Employees) Regulations 1996 apply to employees that are not covered by the 1977 Regulations. The 1996 Regulations require employers to consult their employees on matters which link with the requirements of PUWER 98 and particularly its requirements for information and instruction:

(a)   any measures which may affect their health and safety;

(b)   information they must have about risks to health and safety and preventive measures;

(c)   any arrangements for getting a competent person to help comply with health and safety requirements;

(d)   planning and organising of any health and safety training; and

(e)   the health and safety consequences of any new equipment or technology.

These requirements for consultation link with several of PUWER 98's requirements, for example information, instruction and training on new work equipment.

178   Similar provisions apply offshore under the Offshore Installations (Safety Representatives and Safety Committees) Regulations 1989, which take in additional consultation requirements specific to the offshore sector.

To whom should the information and instructions be made available?

179 You should ensure that any written instructions are available to the people directly using the work equipment. You should also ensure that instructions are made available to other appropriate people, for example maintenance instructions are made available or passed to the people involved in maintaining your work equipment.

180 Supervisors and managers also need access to the information and written instructions. The amount of detailed health and safety information they will need to have immediately available for day-to-day running of production lines will vary but it is important that they know what information is available and where it can be found.

How the information and instructions should be made available

181 Information can be made available in writing, or verbally where it is considered sufficient. It is your responsibility to decide what is appropriate, taking into consideration the individual circumstances. Where there are complicated or unusual circumstances, the information should be in writing. Other factors need to be taken into consideration, such as the degree of skill of the workers involved, their experience and training, the degree of supervision and the complexity and length of the particular job.

182 The information and written instructions should be easy to understand. They should be in clear English and/or other languages if appropriate for the people using them. They should be set out in logical order with illustrations where appropriate. Standard symbols should be used where appropriate.

183 You should give special consideration to any employees with language difficulties or with disabilities which could make it difficult for them to receive or understand the information or instructions. You may need to make special arrangements in these cases.

What the information and instructions should cover

184 Any information and written instructions you provide should cover:

(a) all health and safety aspects arising from the use of the work equipment;

(b) any limitations on these uses;

(c) any foreseeable difficulties that could arise;

(d) the methods to deal with them; and

(e) using any conclusions drawn from experience using the work equipment, you should either record them or take steps to ensure that all appropriate members of the workforce are aware of them.

Regulation 9

Training

(1) Every employer shall ensure that all persons who use work equipment have received adequate training for purposes of health and safety, including training in the methods which may be adopted when using the work equipment, any risks which such use may entail and precautions to be taken.

(2)   Every employer shall ensure that any of his employees who supervises or manages the use of work equipment has received adequate training for purposes of health and safety, including training in the methods which may be adopted when using the work equipment, any risks which such use may entail and precautions to be taken.

What is 'adequate training'?

185   It is not possible to detail here what constitutes 'adequate training' as requirements will vary according to the job or activity and work equipment etc. In general, you will need to:

(a)   evaluate the existing competence of employees to operate the full range of work equipment that they will use;

(b)   evaluate the competence they need to manage or supervise the use of work equipment; and

(c)   train the employee to make up any shortfall between their competence and that required to carry out the work with due regard to health and safety.

186   Account should be taken of the circumstances in which the employee works. For example do they work alone or under close supervision of a competent person?

When is training necessary?

187   Training needs are likely to be greatest on recruitment. However, training needs are also required:

(a)   if the risks to which people are exposed change due to a change in their working tasks; or

(b)   because new technology or equipment is introduced; or

(c)   if the system of work changes.

188   Also, you should provide refresher training if necessary. Skills decline if they are not used regularly. Pay particular attention to people who deputise for others on occasions - as they may need more frequent refresher training than those who do the work regularly.

Training for young people

189   Training and proper supervision of young people is particularly important because of their relative immaturity and unfamiliarity with the working environment. Induction training is of particular importance. There are no general age restrictions in legislation relating to the use of work equipment although there is some ACOP material in the relevant publications dealing with lifting, power presses and wood working; all employees should be competent to use work equipment with due regard to health and safety regardless of their age.

190   The Management Regulations contain specific requirements relating to the employment of young people under the age of 18. These require employers to assess risks to young people before they start work, taking into account their inexperience, lack of awareness of potential risks and their immaturity. Employers must provide information to parents of school-age children (for example when they are on work experience) about the risks and the control

measures introduced and take account of the risk assessment in determining whether the young person should undertake certain work activities.

Other health and safety legislation relating to training

191   PUWER 98 revokes the remaining sector specific law on training in the use of work equipment. The laws that have been removed are listed on pages 72 and 74 of this document.

192   This regulation covers health and safety training related to the provision and use of work equipment. Other health and safety legislation contains general requirements relating to training such as the HSW Act and regulation 11 of the Management Regulations which requires employers to provide employees with general health and safety training. Regulation 9 of PUWER 98 is concerned more specifically with what such training should comprise, ie the precautions to be taken during the use of work equipment.

When should training take place?

193   The Management Regulations specify that health and safety training should take place within working hours.

Driver training

194   **You should ensure that self-propelled work equipment, including any attachments or towed equipment, is only driven by workers who have received appropriate training in the safe driving of such work equipment.**[(o)]

> *(o)   This implements point 2.1 of Annex II of AUWED: 'Self-propelled work equipment shall be driven only by workers who have been appropriately trained in the safe driving of such equipment.'*

Chainsaw operators

195   **All workers who use a chainsaw should be competent to do so. Before using a chainsaw to carry out work on or in a tree, a worker should have received appropriate training and obtained a relevant certificate of competence or national competence award, unless they are undergoing such training and are adequately supervised. However, in the agricultural sector, this requirement only applies to first-time users of a chainsaw.**

196   Portable hand-held chainsaws are dangerous machines which need to be handled with the greatest care. Everyone who uses a chainsaw at work for whatever task must have received adequate training under this regulation. The training should cover:

(a)   dangers arising from the chainsaw itself;

(b)   dangers arising from the task for which the chainsaw is to be used; and

(c)   the precautions to control these dangers, including relevant legal requirements.

197   Over and above this, due to the significant risks involved, if a chainsaw is to be used on or in a tree, the operator will be expected to hold a certificate of competence or national competence award relevant to the work they undertake.

198   The requirement for a certificate or award applies to people working with chainsaws on or in trees on agricultural holdings UNLESS it is done as part of agricultural operations (for example, hedging, clearing fallen branches, or pruning trees to maintain clearance for machines, etc) by the occupier or his employees and they have used a chainsaw before 5 December 1998.

Regulation 10

Conformity with Community requirements

(1)   Every employer shall ensure that an item of work equipment has been designed and constructed in compliance with any essential requirements, that is to say requirements relating to its design or construction in any of the instruments listed in Schedule 1 (being instruments which give effect to Community directives concerning the safety of products).

(2)   Where an essential requirement applied to the design or construction of an item of work equipment, the requirements of regulations 11 to 19 and 22 to 29 shall apply in respect of that item only to the extent that the essential requirement did not apply to it.

(3)   This regulation applies to items of work equipment provided for use in the premises or undertaking of the employer for the first time after 31st December 1992.

What regulation 10 requires

199   This regulation aims to ensure that when work equipment is first provided for use in the workplace after 5 December 1998, it meets certain health and safety requirements. It contains duties that complement those on manufacturers and suppliers in other legislation regarding the initial integrity of equipment.

200   There are legal requirements covering all those involved in the chain of supply of work equipment which are designed to ensure that new work equipment is safe. For example, section 6 of the HSW Act places general duties on designers, manufacturers, importers and suppliers to ensure this so far as is reasonably practicable.

201   Existing legislation on the manufacture and supply of new work equipment is increasingly being supplemented by new and more detailed Regulations implementing EC Directives made under Article 100A of the Treaty of Rome. These new Regulations place duties on the manufacturer and supplier of new work equipment.

Article 100A Directives

202   The aim of Article 100A Directives is to achieve the free movement of goods in the Community Single Market by removing different national controls and harmonising essential health and safety requirements. Examples important to safety at work include the Machinery, the Personal Protective Equipment and the Simple Pressure Vessels Directives.

Essential health and safety requirements

203   Article 100A Directives set out 'essential health and safety requirements' which must be satisfied before products may be sold in the European Economic Area. Products which comply with the Directives must be given free circulation within the European Economic Area. These Directives also apply to equipment

made and put into service in-house. Suppliers must ensure that their products, when placed on the market, comply with the legal requirements implementing the Directives applicable to their product. It is a common feature of these Directives that compliance is claimed by the manufacturer affixing a mark - 'CE Marking' - to the equipment.

204   At present, not all work equipment is covered by a product Directive; nor are product Directives retrospective. However, equipment which was provided for use in the European Economic Area before compliance with the relevant product Directives was required, may need to be modified to comply immediately with regulations 11-24 of PUWER 98.

205   One of the most significant relevant Directives is the Machinery Directive. The Machinery Directive was brought into UK law by the Supply of Machinery (Safety) Regulations 1992 as amended. These Regulations apply to machinery that was first placed on the market after 1 January 1993, though there was a transitional period until 31 December 1994.

206   In practice, regulation 10 means that you will need to check, for example, that adequate operating instructions have been provided with the equipment and that there is information about residual hazards such as noise and vibration. More importantly, you should also check the equipment for obvious faults. Products should also carry a CE marking and be accompanied by relevant certificates or declarations, as required by relevant product Directives. Your supplier should be able to give further advice about what the equipment is designed for and what it can or cannot be used for, or, alternatively make further enquiries about such matters with the manufacturer. Further advice is given in HSE's leaflet *Buying new machinery*.[10]

Regulation 10(1)

207   Regulation 10(1) places a duty on you as users of work equipment. When first providing work equipment for use in the workplace you should ensure that it has been made to the requirements of the legislation implementing any product Directive which is relevant to the equipment. (For interpretation of 'provided for use' see the guidance on regulation 1.) This means that in addition to specifying that work equipment should comply with current health and safety legislation, you should also specify that it should comply with the legislation implementing any relevant EC Directive. Where appropriate, you can check to see that the equipment bears a CE marking and ask for a copy of the EC Declaration of Conformity.

Regulation 10(2)

208   As mentioned in paragraph 19, which sets out the requirements of PUWER, there are certain circumstances where regulations 11-19 and 22-29 will not apply. This can happen when work equipment, first supplied, complies with the applicable parts of the legislation that implements any relevant product Directive. An example of this is the Supply of Machinery (Safety) Regulations 1992 which implement the machinery Directive. Regulations 11-19 and 22-29 do not apply here as this would duplicate the requirements. They WILL apply, however, if they include relevant requirements that are not included in the corresponding product legislation or if that product legislation has not been complied with; for example, if a new machine has been supplied without suitable guards, regulation 11 of PUWER 98 could be used to ensure the user does provide adequate guards.

Dangerous parts of machinery

(1)   *Every employer shall ensure that measures are taken in accordance with paragraph (2) which are effective -*

(a)   *to prevent access to any dangerous part of machinery or to any rotating stock-bar; or*

(b)   *to stop the movement of any dangerous part of machinery or rotating stock-bar before any part of a person enters a danger zone.*

(2)   *The measures required by paragraph (1) shall consist of -*

(a)   *the provision of fixed guards enclosing every dangerous part or rotating stock-bar where and to the extent that it is practicable to do so, but where or to the extent that it is not, then*

(b)   *the provision of other guards or protection devices where and to the extent that it is practicable to do so, but where or to the extent that it is not, then*

(c)   *the provision of jigs, holders, push-sticks or similar protection appliances used in conjunction with the machinery where and to the extent that it is practicable to do so, but where or to the extent that it is not, then*

(d)   *the provision of information, instruction, training and supervision.*

(3)   *All guards and protection devices provided under sub-paragraphs (a) or (b) of paragraph (2) shall -*

(a)   *be suitable for the purpose for which they are provided;*

(b)   *be of good construction, sound material and adequate strength;*

(c)   *be maintained in an efficient state, in efficient working order and in good repair;*

(d)   *not give rise to any increased risk to health or safety;*

(e)   *not be easily bypassed or disabled;*

(f)   *be situated at sufficient distance from the danger zone;*

(g)   *not unduly restrict the view of the operating cycle of the machinery, where such a view is necessary;*

(h)   *be so constructed or adapted that they allow operations necessary to fit or replace parts and for maintenance work, restricting access so that it is allowed only to the area where the work is to be carried out and, if possible, without having to dismantle the guard or protection device.*

(4)   *All protection appliances provided under sub-paragraph (c) of paragraph (2) shall comply with sub-paragraphs (a) to (d) and (g) of paragraph (3).*

(5)   *In this regulation -*

"danger zone" means any zone in or around machinery in which a person is exposed to a risk to health or safety from contact with a dangerous part of machinery or a rotating stock-bar;

"stock-bar" means any part of a stock-bar which projects beyond the head-stock of a lathe.

What regulation 11(1) requires

209   Regulation 11(1) requires employers to take effective measures to prevent access to dangerous parts of machinery or stop their movement before any part of a person enters a danger zone. This regulation also applies to contact with a rotating stock-bar which projects beyond the headstock of a lathe.

210   The term 'dangerous part' has been established in health and safety law through judicial decisions. In practice, this means that if a piece of work equipment could cause injury if it is being used in a foreseeable way, it can be considered a dangerous part.

211   Protection against other hazards associated with machinery is dealt with in regulations 12 and 13. However, the measures required by this regulation may also protect or help to protect against those other hazards such as ejected particles and heat.

Preventing contact with dangerous parts of machinery

212   There are many HSC/HSE publications which are specific to a machine or industry. They describe the measures that can be taken to protect against risks associated with dangerous parts of machinery. Current national, European and international standards may also be used for guidance, where appropriate.

213   Appendix 2 gives more detailed information about the available methods of safeguarding which may be used to conform with regulation 11.

Risk assessment

214   Your risk assessment carried out under regulation 3 of the Management Regulations should identify hazards presented by machinery. Your risk assessment should evaluate the nature of the injury, its severity and likelihood of occurrence for each hazard identified. This will enable you to decide whether the level of risk is acceptable or if risk reduction measures are needed. In most cases the objective of risk reduction measures is to prevent contact of part of the body or clothing with any dangerous part of the machine, for example guarding.

What regulation 11(2) requires

215   Regulation 11(2) specifies the measures which you should take to prevent access to the dangerous parts of the machinery and achieve compliance with regulation 11(1). The measures are ranked in the order they should be implemented, where practicable, to achieve an adequate level of protection. The levels of protection are:

(a)   fixed enclosing guards;

(b)   other guards or protection devices such as interlocked guards and pressure mats;

(c)   protection appliances such as jigs, holders and push-sticks etc; and

(d)   the provision of information, instruction, training and supervision.

An explanation of the guarding and protection terms used is given in Appendix 2.

216 The hazards from machinery will be identified as part of your risk assessment. The purpose of the risk assessment is to identify measures that you can take to reduce the risks that the hazards present. When selecting measures you should consider each level of protection from the first level of the scale listed in paragraph 215 and you should use measures from that level so far as it is practicable to do so, provided that they contribute to the reduction of risk. It may be necessary to select a combination of measures. The selection process should continue down the scale until the combined measures are effective in reducing the risks to an acceptable level thus meeting the requirements of regulation 11(1). In selecting the appropriate combination you will need to take account of the requirements of the work, your evaluation of the risks, and the technical features of possible safeguarding solutions.

217 Most machinery will present more than one mechanical hazard, and you need to deal with the risks associated with all of these. For example, at belt conveyors there is a risk of entanglement with the rotating shafts and of being trapped by the intake between drum and moving belt - so you should adopt appropriate safety measures.

218 Any risk assessment carried out under regulation 3 of the Management Regulations should not just deal with the machine when it is operating normally, but must also cover activities such as setting, maintenance, cleaning or repair. The assessment may indicate that these activities require a different combination of protective measures from those appropriate to the machine doing its normal work. In particular, parts of machinery that are not dangerous in normal use because they are not then accessible may become accessible and therefore dangerous while this type of work is being carried out.

219 Certain setting or adjustment operations which may have to be done with the machine running may require a greater reliance on the provision of information, instruction, training and supervision than for normal use.

Regulation 11(3) and regulation 11(4)

220 Regulation 11(3) sets out various requirements for guards and protection devices which are set out in Appendix 2. These are largely common sense, and in large part are detailed in relevant national, European and international standards. Ways of achieving satisfactory guarding and other protection are discussed in more detail in the standards and in other guidance - see the reference section on page 82. Regulation 11(4) sets out requirements for protection appliances.

Regulation 12   Protection against specified hazards

(1) Every employer shall take measures to ensure that the exposure of a person using work equipment to any risk to his health or safety from any hazard specified in paragraph (3) is either prevented, or, where that is not reasonably practicable, adequately controlled.

(2) The measures required by paragraph (1) shall -

(a) be measures other than the provision of personal protective equipment or of information, instruction, training and supervision, so far as is reasonably practicable; and

42

(b)   include, where appropriate, measures to minimise the effects of the hazard as well as to reduce the likelihood of the hazard occurring.

(3)   The hazards referred to in paragraph (1) are -

(a)   any article or substance falling or being ejected from work equipment;

(b)   rupture or disintegration of parts of work equipment;

(c)   work equipment catching fire or overheating;

(d)   the unintended or premature discharge of any article or of any gas, dust, liquid, vapour or other substance which, in each case, is produced, used or stored in the work equipment;

(e)   the unintended or premature explosion of the work equipment or any article or substance produced, used or stored in it.

(4)   For the purposes of this regulation "adequately" means adequately having regard only to the nature of the hazard and the nature and degree of exposure to the risk.

(5)   This regulation shall not apply where any of the following Regulations apply in respect of any risk to a person's health or safety for which such Regulations require measures to be taken to prevent or control such risk, namely -

(a)   the Ionising Radiations Regulations 1985;[p]

(b)   the Control of Asbestos at Work Regulations 1987;[q]

(c)   the Control of Substances Hazardous to Health Regulations 1994;[r]

(d)   the Noise at Work Regulations 1989;[s]

(e)   the Construction (Head Protection) Regulations 1989;[t]

(f)   the Control of Lead at Work Regulations 1998.[u]

(p) SI 1985/1333, amended by SI 1992/743, 1992/2966.
(q) SI 1987/2115, amended by SI 1988/712, 1992/2966, 1992/3068.
(r) SI 1994/3246, amended by SI 1994/3247, 1996/2001.
(s) SI 1989/1790, amended by SI 1992/2966, 1977/1993.
(t) SI 1989/2209, amended by SI 1992/2966.
(u) SI 1998/543.

What this regulation covers

221   This regulation covers risks arising from hazards during the use of work equipment. The hazards are listed in paragraph (3) of the regulation.

Examples of hazards that the regulation covers are:

(a)   material falling from equipment, for example a loose board falling from scaffolding, a straw bale falling from a tractor foreloader or molten metal spilling from a ladle;

(b)   material held in the equipment being unexpectedly thrown out, for example swarf ejected from a machine tool;

(c)   parts of the equipment breaking off and being thrown out, for example an abrasive wheel bursting;

43

(d)   parts of the equipment coming apart, for example collapse of scaffolding or falsework;

(e)   overheating or fire due, for example, to friction (bearings running hot, conveyor belt on jammed roller), electric motor burning out, thermostat failing, cooling system failure;

(f)   explosion of the equipment due to pressure build-up, perhaps due to the failure of a pressure-relief valve or the unexpected blockage or sealing off of pipework;

(g)   explosion of substances in the equipment, due, for example, to exothermic chemical reaction or unplanned ignition of a flammable gas or vapour or finely divided organic material (for example flour, coal dust), or welding work on a container with flammable residues.

222   Your risk assessment carried out under regulation 3 of the Management Regulations should identify these hazards and assess the risks associated with them. You will need to consider the likelihood of such events occurring and the consequent danger if they do occur, in order to identify measures you should take to comply with this regulation.

223   Regulation 12(1) sets the primary aim, which is to prevent any of the events in regulation 12(3) arising, if that event exposes a person to risk. Where possible, the equipment should be designed so that events presenting a risk cannot occur. If this is not reasonably practicable, you should take steps to reduce the risk. Examples of measures that may be taken are the monitoring of solvent concentrations at evaporating ovens to detect the build-up of explosive atmospheres, or the use of inert gas systems to control and suppress dust explosions.

224   Regulation 12(1) permits the discharge or ejection of material as an intentional or unavoidable part of the process (for example grit-blasting of castings, sawdust from woodworking), but any risks to people must be controlled. The regulation also allows the use of equipment designed to make use of explosive forces in a controlled manner (for example an internal combustion engine or a rail detonator signal).

225   Equipment may have been designed before manufacture to eliminate or reduce the likelihood of the type of event listed in regulation 12(3). But equipment suppliers cannot control the materials used in equipment, or the environment in which it is used, and it is up to you to ensure that the equipment is suitable for their application, as required by regulation 4(2). Therefore risks associated with high temperature, vibration or a flammable atmosphere must be controlled.

226   Regulation 12(2)(b) requires that in addition to reducing the likelihood of the event occurring, measures must be taken to reduce the effect of any event which does give rise to risks. An example might be a blast wall or where there is a risk from a pressure-relief panel or vent bursting, ensuring that any gases or liquids discharged are directed to a safe place, contained, or made safe as appropriate.

227   Regulation 12(2)(a) requires that risk-controlling measures should be provided as part of the equipment, so far as is reasonably practicable. Personal protective equipment may be appropriate where a risk remains that cannot be eliminated in some other way.

228 Training, supervision and provision of information will often have an important role to play. Firstly, they can help to ensure that equipment is operated in the correct way to prevent dangers occurring. Secondly, they can help to ensure that the appropriate safeguards are taken to prevent people being exposed to risk.

Abrasive wheels

229 One particular example of the application of these principles is the use of abrasive wheels.

(a)   To minimise the risk of bursting, abrasive wheels should always be run within the specified maximum rotation speed.

(b)   If they are large enough this will be marked on the wheel (in accordance with regulation 23).

(c)   Smaller wheels should have a notice fixed in the workroom, giving the individual or class maximum permissible rotation speed.

(d)   The power-driven spindle should be governed so that its rotation speed does not exceed this.

(e)   Guarding must be provided to contain fragments of the wheel that might fly off if it did burst, so as to prevent them injuring anyone in the workplace. The guarding has an additional role in helping to meet the requirements of regulation 11; it should be designed, constructed and maintained to fulfil both functions.

(f)   Providing information and training of workers in the correct handling and mounting of abrasive wheels (including pre-mounting and storing procedures) is also necessary to reduce the risk of bursting.

Relationship with other legislation

230 Regulation 12(5) refers to other regulations which cover specific hazards. For example, the Control of Substances Hazardous to Health Regulations (COSHH) would apply to leakage of a toxic substance, whereas regulation 12 would apply to leakage of steam or cooling water from the same equipment. Similarly, COSHH would apply to the discharge of coolant mist from a machine tool, but regulation 12 would apply in the case of ejected swarf.

Regulation 13   High or very low temperature

Every employer shall ensure that work equipment, parts of work equipment and any article or substance produced, used or stored in work equipment which, in each case, is at a high or very low temperature shall have protection where appropriate so as to prevent injury to any person by burn, scald or sear.

231 Regulation 13 deals with the risk of injury from contact with hot or very cold work equipment, parts of work equipment or articles or substances in the work equipment. It does not cover any related risk such as radiant heat or glare.

232 Accessible surfaces of equipment or machinery, when hot or very cold, represent sources of risk of burn or other injury such as frostbite. Examples of

relevant equipment might include a flat-iron, foundry equipment, drop forging, hot pressing, liquid nitrogen tank, gas cooker, blast furnace, snow-making machine, cold store, steam pipe, etc and employees may have to work close to the equipment. Touching such surfaces may take place intentionally, for example to operate a handle of the equipment, or unintentionally, when someone is near the equipment. In many cases, surfaces of equipment or devices have to be hot and accessible to operate, for example cooker hotplates, soldering iron bit, heated rolls. In such cases no engineering protective measures can be taken.

233 You should reduce the risk from contact with hot surfaces by engineering methods, ie reduction of surface temperature, insulation, shielding, barricading and guarding. The risk from hot process materials - contact, splashing, spilling, etc - should likewise be reduced by limiting maximum temperature, limiting liquor level, indirect steam heating methods, provision of doors, lids or covers, temperature interlocking of doors or lids and deflection systems for hot liquor (catch pan, spillway, etc).

234 In cases in which engineering protective measures can be applied, for example by reducing surface temperatures, you should adopt these in preference to personal protective measures. You will need to decide the choice of protective measures in each particular case and according to the particular circumstances.

235 While engineering measures should always be applied where appropriate, alternative or complementary forms of protection may also be necessary. For example, these could include the use of personal protective equipment (see the Personal Protective Equipment at Work Regulations 1992) and/or organisational measures such as warning signs (warning signals, visual and noise alarm signals), instructions, training, supervision, technical documentation, operating instructions, instructions for use.

Regulations 14 to 18 - Controls and control systems

Controls for starting or making a significant change in operating conditions

236 Regulations 14 to 18 require the provision of controls 'where appropriate'. This qualification relates both to the features and functioning of the work equipment itself and to whether there is a risk associated with its use.

237 The Regulations on controls and control systems apply not only to equipment with moving parts such as machinery, but may also apply to other equipment which might create a risk, such as ovens, X-ray generators, and lasers.

238 Start, stop and emergency stop controls are not generally appropriate where work equipment has no moving parts. Similarly, they are not appropriate where the risk of injury is negligible such as, for example, battery-powered clocks or solar-powered calculators.

239 Some types of work equipment are manually powered and although their use involves risk of injury, human control makes the provision of controls inappropriate. Examples include the following when they use only manual power:

46

(a)   guillotines;

(b)   hand-drills;

(c)   lawn-mowers.

240   Some types of manually-powered work equipment may need stop controls, if it does not come to a halt when the human effort stops.

241   A control is the manual actuator that the operator touches, for example a button, foot-pedal, knob, or lever. Normally it is part of a control device such as a brake, clutch, switch, or relay. The control and control device are parts of the control system which may be considered as all the components which act together to monitor and control the functions of the work equipment. Control systems may operate using mechanical linkages, electricity, pneumatics, hydraulics etc, or combinations of these.

242   In practice, most individual items of equipment are likely to be provided with appropriate controls when supplied.

243   For complex items of equipment, installations or assemblies comprising several different items of equipment, it may be necessary to carry out a more detailed assessment of the risks and make special provisions to ensure that controls are provided that comply fully with these Regulations.

Regulation 14

Controls for starting or making a significant change in operating conditions

(1)   Every employer shall ensure that, where appropriate, work equipment is provided with one or more controls for the purposes of -

(a)   starting the work equipment (including re-starting after a stoppage for any reason); or

(b)   controlling any change in the speed, pressure or other operating conditions of the work equipment where such conditions after the change result in risk to health and safety which is greater than or of a different nature from such risks before the change.

(2)   Subject to paragraph (3), every employer shall ensure that, where a control is required by paragraph (1), it shall not be possible to perform any operation mentioned in sub-paragraph (a) or (b) of that paragraph except by a deliberate action on such control.

(3)   Paragraph (1) shall not apply to re-starting or changing operating conditions as a result of the normal operating cycle of an automatic device.

244   It should only be possible to start the equipment by using appropriate controls. Operating the control need not necessarily immediately start the equipment as control systems may require certain conditions (for example, those relating to operation or protection devices) to be met before starting can be achieved.

245   Restarting the equipment after any stoppage is subject to the same requirements. The stoppage may have been deliberate or may have happened, for example, by the activation of a protection device. You should not normally be able to restart the equipment simply by re-setting a protection device such as, for example, an interlock or a person's withdrawal from an area covered by a sensing device - operation of the start control should also be required.

246 Any change in the operating conditions of the equipment should only be possible by the use of a control unless the change does not increase risks to health and safety. Examples of operating conditions include speed, pressure, temperature and power. For example, certain multifunctional machines are used in the metal working industry for punching or shearing metal using different tools located on different parts of the machines. Safety in the use of these machines is achieved by means of a combination of safe systems of work and physical safeguards which match the characteristics of the workpiece. It is essential that the function of the machine (for example punching or shearing) is changed by a conscious, positive action by the operator and that unused parts of the machine cannot start up unintentionally.

Regulation 14(1)(b) and 14(2)

247 The purpose of regulation 14(1)(b) and 14(2) is to ensure that users or other people are not caught unawares by any changes in the operating conditions or modes of the equipment in use.

Regulation 14(3)

248 Regulation 14(3) acknowledges that in the case of automatic machinery such as those controlled by programmable electronic systems, it is not appropriate to require separate controls for changing operating conditions when such changes are part of the normal operating cycle. (Nevertheless, these machines should be safeguarded as required by regulations 11 and 12.) However, where you need to make interventions outside the normal sequence, such as clearing blockages, setting or cleaning, you should provide proper controls in accordance with regulations 14(1) and (2).

249 The start control can be separate, combined with controls for operating conditions, or more than one of each type of control can be provided. The controls can be combined with stop controls as required by regulation 15 but not with an emergency stop control provided in accordance with regulation 16. 'Hold-to-run' devices are examples of combined stop and start controls. These should be designed so that the stop function has priority following the release of the control.

250 The controls provided should be designed and positioned so as to prevent, so far as possible, inadvertent or accidental operation. Buttons or levers, for example, should have an appropriate shrouding or locking facility. It should not be possible for the control to 'operate itself', for example due to the effects of gravity, vibration or failure of a spring mechanism. Starting that is initiated from a keyboard or other multifunction device should require some form of confirmation in addition to the start command. Furthermore, the results of the actuation should be displayed.

Regulation 15

Stop controls

(1)   Every employer shall ensure that, where appropriate, work equipment is provided with one or more readily accessible controls the operation of which will bring the work equipment to a safe condition in a safe manner.

(2)   Any control required by paragraph (1) shall bring the work equipment to a complete stop where necessary for reasons of health and safety.

(3)   Any control required by paragraph (1) shall, if necessary for reasons of health and safety, switch off all sources of energy after stopping the functioning of the work equipment.

(4)   Any control required by paragraph (1) shall operate in priority to any control which starts or changes the operating conditions of the work equipment.

251   Regulation 15(1) requires that the action of the stop control should bring the equipment to a safe condition in a safe manner. This acknowledges that it is not always desirable to bring all items of work equipment immediately to a complete stop if this could result in other risks. For example, stopping the mixing mechanism of a reactor during certain chemical reactions could lead to a dangerous exothermic reaction.

252   The stop control does not have to be instantaneous in its action and can bring the equipment to rest in sequence or at the end of an operating cycle if this is required for safety. This may be necessary in some processes, for example to prevent the unsafe build-up of heat or pressure or to allow a controlled run-down of large rotating parts with high inertia.

253   Regulation 15(2) is qualified by 'where necessary for reasons of health and safety'. Therefore all accessible dangerous parts must be rendered stationary which may mean they need to be locked into position and may be allowed to idle. However, parts of equipment which do not present a risk, such as suitably guarded cooling fans, do not need to be positively stopped.

254   Regulation 15(3) requires that the control should switch off all sources of energy from the equipment, after it has stopped, if this is necessary to prevent or minimise risk to health or safety. Where it is necessary to retain power for production reasons and a hazard could arise due to unexpected movement giving rise to risk of injury, control systems should be designed so as to immediately remove the power, should such an event occur. Where internally stored energy could lead to risk, it should be cut off by the action of the stop control. For example, horizontal plastic injection moulding machines may store hydraulic energy in internal hydraulic reservoirs which, under certain fault conditions, may cause uncovenanted movements which could cause injury. In this case, the stop control should effectively isolate or dissipate the stored energy so as to ensure safety.

255   The stop control should take priority over any operating or start control. Where possible, it should not require anything other than a short manual action to activate it, even though the stop and disconnection sequence so initiated may take some time to complete. Further information on the categories of stop function can be found in BS EN 60204-1. Although this standard (which deals with specifications for general requirements for an individual machine) applies to new machinery, it gives valuable guidance which may be useful for any equipment - new or used.

Regulation 16

Emergency stop controls

(1)   Every employer shall ensure that, where appropriate, work equipment is provided with one or more readily accessible emergency stop controls unless it is not necessary by reason of the nature of the hazards and the time taken for the work equipment to come to a complete stop as a result of the action of any control provided by virtue of regulation 15(1).

(2)   Any control required by paragraph (1) shall operate in priority to any control required by regulation 15(1).

256 An emergency stop control should be provided where the other safeguards in place are not adequate to prevent risk when an irregular event occurs. However, an emergency stop control should not be considered as a substitute for safeguarding.

257 Where it is appropriate to have one, based on the risk assessment, you should provide an emergency stop at every control point and at other appropriate locations around the equipment so that action can be taken quickly. The location of emergency stop controls should be determined as a follow-up to the risk assessment required under the Management Regulations. Although it is desirable that emergency stops rapidly bring work equipment to a halt, this must be achieved under control so as not to create any additional hazards.

258 As emergency stops are intended to effect a rapid response to potentially dangerous situations, they should not be used as functional stops during normal operation.

259 Emergency stop controls should be easily reached and actuated. Common types are mushroom-headed buttons, bars, levers, kick-plates, or pressure-sensitive cables. Guidance on specific features of emergency stops is given in national, European and international standards.

Regulation 17   Controls

(1) Every employer shall ensure that all controls for work equipment are clearly visible and identifiable, including by appropriate marking where necessary.

(2) Except where necessary, the employer shall ensure that no control for work equipment is in a position where any person operating the control is exposed to a risk to his health or safety.

(3) Every employer shall ensure where appropriate -

(a) that, so far as is reasonably practicable, the operator of any control is able to ensure from the position of that control that no person is in a place where he would be exposed to any risk to his health or safety as a result of the operation of that control, but where or to the extent that it is not reasonably practicable;

(b) that, so far as is reasonably practicable, systems of work are effective to ensure that, when work equipment is about to start, no person is in a place where he would be exposed to a risk to his health or safety as a result of the work equipment starting, but where neither of these is reasonably practicable;

(c) that an audible, visible or other suitable warning is given by virtue of regulation 24 whenever work equipment is about to start.

(4) Every employer shall take appropriate measures to ensure that any person who is in a place where he would be exposed to a risk to his health or safety as a result of the starting or stopping of work equipment has sufficient time and suitable means to avoid that risk.

Regulation 17(1)

260 It should be possible to identify easily what each control does and on which equipment it takes effect. Both the controls and their markings should be clearly visible. As well as having legible wording or symbols, factors such as the

colour, shape and position of controls are important; a combination of these can often be used to reduce ambiguity. Some controls may need to be distinguishable by touch, for example inching buttons on printing machines. Few controls will be adequately identifiable without marking of some sort.

261   The marking and form of many controls is covered by national, European and international standards either generic or specific to the type of equipment (BS 3641, prEN 50099). However, additional marking may often be desirable.

Regulation 17(2)

262   Controls used in the normal running of the equipment should normally not be placed where anybody using them might be exposed to risk. However, controls used for setting-up and fault-finding procedures may have to be positioned where people are at some risk, for example on a robot-teaching pendant. In such cases particular precautions should be employed to ensure safety; examples include using hold-to-run controls, enabling controls, emergency stop controls. Further precautions include the selection of reduced/limited capability of the work equipment during such operations.

Regulation 17(3)(a)

263   The provisions of regulation 17(3)(a) apply where physical safeguarding methods employed in accordance with regulation 11(2)(a) and (b) do not completely prevent access to dangerous parts of work equipment, or where people are at risk from other aspects of the operation, eg noise, or harmful radiation. The preferred aim is to position controls so that operators of equipment are able to see from the control position that no one is at risk from anything they set going. To be able to do this, operators need to have a view of any part of the equipment that may put anyone at risk. A direct view is best, but supplementing by mirrors or more sophisticated visual or sensing facilities may be necessary.

264   There will normally be little difficulty in meeting this requirement in the case of small and compact equipment. With larger equipment there is normally some latitude in the positioning of controls, and the safety aspect should be considered in deciding their location; this would apply, for example, on large process plant such as newspaper printing machinery or chemical plant.

265   Where people are at risk from dangerous parts of machinery, normal safeguarding procedures should restrict the need for surveillance to vulnerable areas; an example would be on large newspaper printing machines. However, where regular intervention is necessary, which involves entry into, removal of, or opening of safeguards, for example for maintenance purposes, interlocks or similar devices may be necessary as appropriate to prevent start-up while people are at risk. You may need to employ additional measures to ensure that people do not remain inside safeguards at start-up. Similarly, where sensing devices are employed to aid surveillance, they may be interlocked with the controls so as to prevent start-up when people are at risk.

266   If anyone other than the operator is also working on the equipment, they may use permissive start controls. Such controls can indicate to the operator that everyone is clear and permit a start. These can be located at a position of safety from where they can ascertain that no one is at risk.

267   Where there is a risk other than from dangerous parts of machinery (for example noise, radiation), people at some distance from the work equipment may be affected. In such circumstances, it may not always be reasonably

51

practicable for operators to have sight of all parts of the work equipment so it may be necessary to employ systems of work or warning devices. Warning devices only provide limited protection and additional measures may be required if the risks are high. For example, it would not be acceptable to rely on audible or visible alarms where the risk is of an imminent potentially fatal dose of ionising radiation, but they may be adequate where the risk is from noisy plant.

Regulation 17(3)(b)

268   If the nature of the installation is such that it is not reasonably practicable for the operator at the control position to ensure that no one is at risk, then a system of work must be devised and used to achieve that aim. This should implement procedures to eliminate or reduce the probability of any workers being at risk as a result of starting-up. An example is the use of systems using signallers; these are often used to assist crane drivers, or tractor drivers setting a manned harvester in motion.

Regulation 17(3)(c)

269   The warning should comply with regulation 24, ie it should be unambiguous, easily perceived and easily understood. Signals may be visual, audible, tactile or a combination of the three, as appropriate.

Regulation 17(4)

270   Warnings given in accordance with regulation 17(3)(c) should be given sufficiently in advance of the equipment actually starting to give those at risk time to get clear or take suitable actions to prevent risks. This may take the form of a device by means of which the person at risk can prevent start-up or warn the operator of their presence.

271   The provisions of regulation 17 do not preclude people from remaining in positions where they are at risk. Their aim is to prevent an operator unintentionally placing people at risk. Regulation 11, in its hierarchical approach to safeguarding, recognises that in exceptional circumstances people may have to approach dangerous parts of machinery, such as for maintenance purposes. Access to such positions should only be allowed under strictly controlled conditions and in accordance with regulation 11.

Regulation 18   Control systems

(1)   Every employer shall -

(a)   ensure, so far as is reasonably practicable, that all control systems of work equipment are safe; and

(b)   are chosen making due allowance for the failures, faults and constraints to be expected in the planned circumstances of use.

(2)   Without prejudice to the generality of paragraph (1), a control system shall not be safe unless -

(a)   its operation does not create any increased risk to health or safety;

(b)   it ensures, so far as is reasonably practicable, that any fault in or damage to any part of the control system or the loss of supply of any source of energy used by the work equipment cannot result in additional or increased risk to health or safety;

(c)   it does not impede the operation of any control required by regulation 15 or 16.

272   Another way of defining a control system is:

'a control system is a system or device which responds to input signals and generates an output signal which causes the equipment under control to operate in a particular manner.'

273   The input signals may be made by an operator via a manual control, or from the equipment itself, for example from automatic sensors or protection devices (photoelectric guards, guard interlock devices, speed limiters, etc). Signals from the equipment may also include information (feedback) on the condition of the equipment and its response (position, whether it is running, speed).

274   Failure of any part of the control system or its power supply should lead to a 'fail-safe' condition. Fail-safe can also be more correctly and realistically called 'minimised failure to danger'. This should not impede the operation of the 'stop' or 'emergency stop' controls. The measures which should be taken in the design and application of a control system to mitigate against the effects of its failure will need to be balanced against the consequences of any failure. The greater the risk, the more resistant the control system should be to the effects of failure. Bringing a machine to a safe halt may achieve the objective. Halting a chemical process, however, could create further hazards. Care should be taken to fully assess the consequences of such events and provide further protection, ie standby power plant or diverting chemicals to a place of safety. It should always be possible to recover to a safe condition.

275   There are national, European and international standards both current and in preparation (BS EN 60204- 1, BS EN 954-1) which provide guidance on design of control systems so as to achieve high levels of performance related to safety. Though they are aimed at new machinery, they may be used as guidance for existing work equipment.

Regulation 19   Isolation from sources of energy

(1)   Every employer shall ensure that where appropriate work equipment is provided with suitable means to isolate it from all its sources of energy.

(2)   Without prejudice to the generality of paragraph (1), the means mentioned in that paragraph shall not be suitable unless they are clearly identifiable and readily accessible.

(3)   Every employer shall take appropriate measures to ensure that re-connection of any energy source to work equipment does not expose any person using the work equipment to any risk to his health or safety.

276   The main aim of this regulation is to allow equipment to be made safe under particular circumstances, such as when maintenance is to be carried out, when an unsafe condition develops (failure of a component, overheating, or pressure build-up), or where a temporarily adverse environment would render

the equipment unsafe, for example electrical equipment in wet conditions or in a flammable or explosive atmosphere.

277   Isolation means establishing a break in the energy supply in a secure manner, ie by ensuring that inadvertent reconnection is not possible. You should identify the possibilities and risks of reconnection as part of your risk assessment, which should then establish how secure isolation can be achieved. For some equipment, this can be done by simply removing the plug from the electrical supply socket. For other equipment, an isolating switch or valve may have to be locked in the off or closed position to avoid unsafe reconnection. The closed position is not always the safe position: for example, drain or vent outlets may need to be secured in the open position.

278   If work on isolated equipment is being done by more than one person, it may be necessary to provide a locking device with multiple locks and keys. Each will have their own lock or key, and all locks have to be taken off before the isolating device can be removed. Keys should not be passed to anyone other than the nominated personnel and should not be interchanged between nominated people.

279   For safety reasons in some circumstances, sources of energy may need to be maintained when the equipment is stopped, for example when the power supply is helping to keep the equipment or parts of it safe. In such cases, isolation could lead to consequent danger, so it will be necessary to take appropriate measures to eliminate any risk before attempting to isolate the equipment.

280   It is appropriate to provide means of isolation where the work equipment is dependent upon external energy sources such as electricity, pressure (hydraulic or pneumatic) or heat. Where possible, means of dissipating stored energy should be provided. Other sources of energy such as its potential energy, chemical or radiological energy, cannot be isolated from the equipment. Nevertheless, there should be a means of preventing such energy from adversely affecting workers, by shielding, barriers or restraint.

281   Isolation of electrical equipment is dealt with by regulation 12 of the Electricity at Work Regulations 1989. Guidance to those Regulations expands on the means of isolating electrical equipment. Note that those Regulations are only concerned with electrical danger (electric shock or burn, arcing and fire or explosion caused by electricity), and do not deal with other risks (such as mechanical) that may arise from failure to isolate electrical equipment.

282   Thermal energy may be supplied by circulation of pre-heated fluid such as water or steam. In such cases, isolating valves should be fitted to the supply pipework.

283   Similar provision should be made for energy supplies in the form of liquids or gases under pressure. A planned preventive maintenance programme should therefore be instigated which assures effective means of isolation. It may be necessary to isolate pipework by physically disconnecting it or fitting spades in the line to provide the necessary level of protection. Redundancy in the form of more than one isolation valve fitted in series may also be used, but care should be exercised to check the efficacy of each valve function periodically. The performance of such valves may deteriorate over time, and their effectiveness often cannot be judged visually.

284   The energy source of some equipment is held in the substances contained within it; examples are the use of gases or liquids as fuel, electrical accumulators

(batteries) and radionuclides. In such cases, isolation may mean removing the energy-containing material, although this may not always be necessary.

285 Also, it is clearly not appropriate to isolate the terminals of a battery from the chemical cells within it, since that could not be done without destroying the whole unit.

286 Some equipment makes use of natural sources of energy such as light or flowing water. In such cases, suitable means of isolation include screening from light, and the means of diverting water flow, respectively. Another natural energy source, wind power, is less easily diverted, so sail mechanisms should be designed and constructed so as to permit minimal energy transfer when necessary. Effective restraint should be provided to prevent uncovenanted movement when taken out of use for repair or maintenance.

287 Regulation 19(3) requires precautions to ensure that people are not put at risk following reconnection of the energy source. So, reconnection of the energy source should not put people at risk by itself initiating movement or other hazard. Measures are also required to ensure that guards and other protection devices are functioning correctly before operation begins.

Regulation 20 — Stability

Every employer shall ensure that work equipment or any part of work equipment is stabilised by clamping or otherwise where necessary for purposes of health or safety.

288 There are many types of work equipment that might fall over, collapse or overturn unless suitable precautions are taken to fix them to the ground by bolting, tying, fastening or clamping them in some way and/or to stabilise them by ballasting or counterbalancing. Where ballasting or counterbalancing is employed for portable equipment, you should reappraise the stabilising method each time the equipment is repositioned.

289 Most machines used in a fixed position should be bolted or otherwise fastened down so that they do not move or rock during use. This can be done by fastening the equipment to an appropriate foundation or supporting structure. Other means could include lashing or tying to a supporting structure or platform.

290 Where the stability of the work equipment is not inherent in its design or operation or where it is mounted in a position where its stability could be compromised, for example by severe weather conditions, additional measures should be taken to ensure its stability. Ladders should be at the correct angle, and tied or footed.

291 Certain types of mobile work equipment, for example access platforms, while inherently stable, can have their stability increased during use by means of outriggers or similar devices. While this equipment cannot be 'clamped' or 'fixed', steps must be taken to ensure that the equipment is always used within the limits of its stability at any given time.

Regulation 21   Lighting

PUWER 98

Regulation 21

PUWER 98

Every employer shall ensure that suitable and sufficient lighting, which takes account of the operations to be carried out, is provided at any place where a person uses work equipment.

292   Any place where a person uses work equipment should be suitably and sufficiently lit. If the ambient lighting provided in the workplace is suitable and sufficient for the tasks involved in the use of the equipment, special lighting need not be provided. But if the task involves the perception of detail, for example precision measurements, you would need to provide additional lighting to comply with the regulation. The lighting should be adequate for the needs of the task.

293   You should provide local lighting on the machine for the illumination of the work area when the construction of the machine and/or its guards render the normal lighting inadequate for the safe and efficient operation of the machine, for example on sewing machines. Local lighting may be needed to give sufficient view of a dangerous process or to reduce visual fatigue. Travelling cranes may obscure overhead lighting for the driver and others, particularly when there is no natural light available (nightworking), and supplementary lighting may be necessary.

294   You should also provide additional lighting in areas not covered by general lighting when work, such as maintenance or repairs, for example, is carried out in them. The arrangements for the provision of lighting could be temporary, by means of hand or other portable lights, for example by fixed lighting inside enclosures, such as lift shafts. The standard of lighting required will be related to the purpose for which the work equipment is used or to the work being carried out. Lighting levels should be checked periodically to ensure that the intensity is not diminished by dust and grime deposits. Where necessary, you should clean luminaires and reflectors at regular intervals to maintain lighting efficiency.

295   Where access is foreseeable on an intermittent but regular basis, you should always consider providing permanent lighting.

296   This regulation complements the requirement for sufficient and suitable workplace lighting in the Workplace (Health, Safety and Welfare) Regulations 1992 and the Electricity at Work Regulations 1989. Guidance is contained in HSE's guidance *Lighting at work*.[11]

Guidance 21

Regulation 22   Maintenance operations

PUWER 98

Every employer shall take appropriate measures to ensure that work equipment is so constructed or adapted that, so far as is reasonably practicable, maintenance operations which involve a risk to health or safety can be carried out while the work equipment is shut down, or in other cases -

(a)   maintenance operations can be carried out without exposing the person carrying them out to a risk to his health or safety; or

(b)   appropriate measures can be taken for the protection of any person carrying out maintenance operations which involve a risk to his health or safety.

Regulation 22

297 Regulation 5 requires that equipment is maintained. Regulation 22 requires that equipment is constructed or adapted in a way that takes account of the risks associated with carrying out maintenance work, such as routine and planned preventive maintenance, as described in the guidance to regulation 5. Compliance with this regulation will help to ensure that when maintenance work is carried out, it is possible to do it safely and without risk to health, as required by Section 2 of the HSW Act; it will also help to comply with regulation 5(1), since 'used' includes maintained. Regulation 11(3)(h) contains a requirement linked to regulation 22, but focusing on the narrower aspect of the design of guards for such work. Many accidents have occurred during maintenance work, often as a result of failure to adapt the equipment to reduce the risk.

298 In most cases the need for safe maintenance will have been considered at the design stage and attended to by the manufacturer, and you will need to do little other than review the measures provided. In other cases, particularly when a range of interconnecting components may be put together, for example in a research laboratory or a production line, you will need to consider when carrying out your risk assessment whether any extra features need to be incorporated so that maintenance can be done safely and without risks to health.

299 Ideally, there is no risk associated with the maintenance operation. For example, lubrication points on machines may be designed so that they can be accessed safely even while the machine is in motion, or adjustment points positioned so that they can be used without opening guards.

300 If, however, the maintenance work might involve a risk, this regulation requires that the installation should be designed so that the work can, so far as is reasonably practicable, be carried out with the equipment stopped or inactive. This will probably be the case for most equipment.

301 If equipment will have to be running or working during a maintenance operation and this presents risks, you should take measures to enable the operation of the equipment in a way that reduces the risk. These measures include further safeguards or functions designed into the equipment, such as limiting the power, speed or range of movement that is available to dangerous parts or providing protection during maintenance operations. Examples are:

(a)   providing temporary guards;

(b)   limited movement controls;

(c)   crawl speed operated by hold-to-run controls;

(d)   using a second low-powered visible laser beam to align a powerful invisible one.

302 Other measures that can be taken to protect against any residual risk include wearing personal protective equipment and provision of instruction and supervision. Although the actual use of these measures falls outside the scope of this regulation, the work equipment should as far as possible be installed to be compatible with their use.

303 The design of equipment in relation to maintenance work on it may also be affected by other legislation. In particular, electrically powered equipment is subject to the Electricity at Work Regulations 1989 as regards risks of injury from electric shock or burn, or from explosion or ignition initiated by electricity. Guidance on those Regulations includes details of relevant equipment requirements.

Regulation 23   Markings

**PUWER 98
Regulation 23**

Every employer shall ensure that work equipment is marked in a clearly visible manner with any marking appropriate for reasons of health and safety.

PUWER 98

304   This regulation is closely related to the following one which deals with warnings; some markings may also serve as the warning required by regulation 24. There are many circumstances in which marking of equipment is appropriate for health or safety reasons. Stop and start controls for equipment need to be identified. The maximum rotation speed of an abrasive wheel should be marked upon it. The maximum safe working load (rated capacity) should be marked on lifting equipment. Gas cylinders should indicate (normally by colour) the gas in them. Storage and feed vessels containing hazardous substances should be marked to show their contents, and any hazard associated with them. Pipework for water and compressed air and other mains services should be colour-coded to indicate contents.

305   Some legislation lays down specific circumstances in which markings are needed, and what form they should take. Examples of Regulations requiring particular markings are the Ionising Radiation Regulations 1985, and the Highly Flammable Liquids and Liquefied Petroleum Gases Regulations 1972 (regulations 6 and 7). Pressure vessels are subject to various Regulations, which include requirements for marking the vessel with specific information.

306   You should consider any other marking that might be appropriate for your own purposes, for example numbering machines to aid identification, particularly if the controls or isolators for the machines are not directly attached to them and there could otherwise be confusion.

307   Markings may use words, letters, numbers, or symbols, and the use of colour or shape may be significant. There are nationally or internationally agreed markings relating to some hazards, for example the international symbols for radiation and lasers. Markings should as far as possible conform to such published standards as BS 5378 or as required by any appropriate legislation such as the Health and Safety (Safety Signs and Signals) Regulations 1996.

Guidance 23

Regulation 24   Warnings

PUWER 98

Regulation 24

(1)   Every employer shall ensure that work equipment incorporates any warnings or warning devices which are appropriate for reasons of health and safety.

(2)   Without prejudice to the generality of paragraph (1), warnings given by warning devices on work equipment shall not be appropriate unless they are unambiguous, easily perceived and easily understood.

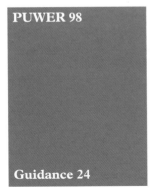

PUWER 98

308   Warnings or warning devices may be appropriate where risks to health or safety remain after other hardware measures have been taken. They may be incorporated into systems of work (including permit-to-work systems), and can enforce measures of information, instruction and training. A warning is normally in the form of a notice or similar. Examples are positive instructions ('hard hats must be worn'), prohibitions ('not to be operated by people under 18 years'), restrictions ('do not heat above 60°C'). A warning device is an active unit giving a signal; the signal may typically be visible or audible, and is often connected into equipment so that it is active only when a hazard exists.

Guidance 24

309   In some cases, warnings and warning devices will be specified in other

legislation, for example automatic safe load indicators on mobile cranes on construction sites, or 'X-rays on' lights.

Warnings

310   Warnings can be permanent printed ones; these may be attached to or incorporated into the equipment or positioned close to it. There may also be a need for portable warnings to be posted during temporary operations such as maintenance; these may form part of a permit-to-work system.

311   In some cases words can be augmented or replaced by appropriate graphical signs. So as to be readily understood, such signs will normally need to be from a nationally or internationally agreed standard set. The Health and Safety (Safety Signs and Signals) Regulations 1996 are relevant here.

312   Warning devices can be:

(a)   audible, for example reversing alarms on construction vehicles;

(b)   visible, for example a light on a control panel that a fan on a microbiological cabinet has broken down or a blockage has occurred on a particular machine;

(c)   an indication of imminent danger, for example machine about to start, or development of a fault condition (ie pump failure or conveyor blockage indicator on a control panel); or

(d)   the continued presence of a potential hazard (for example, hotplate or laser on).

A particular warning may use both types of device simultaneously, for example, some automatic safe load indicators on mobile cranes.

313   Warnings must be easily perceived and understood, and unambiguous. It is important to consider factors which affect people's perception of such devices, especially for warnings of imminent danger. Visual warnings will be effective only if a person frequently looks in a particular direction, and therefore may not be as widely applicable as audible signals. Appropriate choice of colour and flashing can catch attention, and also reinforce the warning nature of a visual signal. The sound given by an audible signal should be of such a type that people unambiguously perceive it as a warning. This means that it must be possible to distinguish between the warnings given by separate warning devices and between the warnings and any other, unrelated, signals which may be in operation at the time. It may not be possible to rely on audible signals in a noisy environment, nor in circumstances where many such signals are expected to be active at one time.

PUWER 98 - REGULATIONS 25-30

PART III: MOBILE WORK EQUIPMENT

Introduction

314   Part III is additional to the other requirements of PUWER 98 (such as training, guarding and inspection) which apply to all work equipment including mobile work equipment. The regulations in Part III of PUWER 98 implement

additional requirements for mobile work equipment, which relate to the equipment when it is travelling. Except for the specific requirements of regulation 30 which deals with drive shafts, they are not intended to apply to moving parts of mobile work equipment which is carrying out work in a static position, for example an excavator involved in digging operations.

315 Some of these requirements build on the requirements of the Health and Safety at Work etc Act 1974 (HSW Act) and its supporting ACOP and guidance material that appears at paragraphs 31 to 54 of this publication.

316 Where vehicles are designed primarily for travel on public roads, compliance with the Road Vehicles (Construction and Use) Regulations 1986 will normally be sufficient to comply with the Regulations in Part III of PUWER 98.

317 New mobile work equipment taken into use from 5 December 1998 should comply with all the requirements of PUWER 98. Existing work equipment does not need to comply with Part III of PUWER 98 until 5 December 2002 (see paragraph 57).

What is mobile work equipment?

318 For the purposes of PUWER 98 (Part III), mobile work equipment is any work equipment which carries out work while it is travelling or which travels between different locations where it is used to carry out work. Such equipment would normally be moved on, for example wheels, tracks, rollers, skids, etc. Mobile work equipment may be self-propelled, towed or remote controlled and may incorporate attachments.

Self-propelled mobile work equipment

319 Self-propelled mobile work equipment is work equipment which is propelled by its own motor or mechanism. The motor or mechanism may be powered by energy generated on the mobile work equipment itself, for example by an internal combustion engine, or through connection to a remote power source, such as an electric cable, electric induction or hydraulic line.

Attachment

320 Attachments are work equipment which may be mounted on self-propelled mobile work equipment to alter its characteristics. For example, a load rotator fitted to a fork-lift truck will alter its load-handling capabilities and may alter its safety characteristics, such as stability. Attachments are not considered to be mobile work equipment in their own right but if they can affect the safety of the self-propelled mobile work equipment when they are attached, they are considered to be part of the self-propelled work equipment. Attachments may be non-powered, powered by an independent power source or powered by the self-propelled work equipment to which they are attached.

Towed mobile work equipment

321 Towed mobile work equipment includes work equipment such as towed machines and trailers which are primarily self-supporting on, for example, their own wheels. They may have moving parts which are:

(a)   powered by the vehicle (for example, a power harrow);

(b)   an integral power source (for example, a powered crop sprayer); or

60

(c) they may have no moving parts and function as a result of the movement of the mobile work equipment (for example, a plough or trailer).

Remote-controlled mobile work equipment

322   For the purposes of PUWER 98, remote-controlled mobile work equipment is operated by controls which are not physically connected to it, for example radio control.

Pedestrian-controlled work equipment

323   You should note that pedestrian-controlled work equipment, for example, a lawn-mower, is not likely to be covered by the Regulations in Part III of PUWER 98 irrespective of whether some functions are powered or not.

APPLICATION OF PART III

Regulation 25

Employees carried on mobile work equipment

Every employer shall ensure that no employee is carried by mobile work equipment unless-

(a)   it is suitable for carrying persons; and

(b)   it incorporates features for reducing to as low as is reasonably practicable risks to their safety, including risks from wheels or tracks.

324   You should ensure that risks to the operator and other workers due to the mobile work equipment travelling are controlled. Workers should be protected against falling out of the equipment and from unexpected movement.

When regulation 25 applies

325   Regulation 25 contains general requirements which cover the risks to people (drivers, operators and passengers) carried by mobile work equipment when it is travelling. This includes risks associated with people falling from the equipment or from unexpected movement while it is in motion or stopping. It also covers risks associated with the environment and the place in which the mobile work equipment is used (for example, falling objects, low roofs and the surfaces on which it operates). Regulations 26-30 deal with particular risks.

326   Regulation 25(b) also specifically covers the risks from wheels and tracks when the equipment is travelling but it does not cover the risks from other moving parts, which are covered by regulation 11. In addition, it does not cover the risks associated with mounting or dismounting from the equipment which is covered by the HSW Act.

Suitable for carrying people

327   Operator stations with seats or work platforms normally provide a secure place on which the drivers and other people can travel on mobile work equipment.

Seating

328 Seats should be provided wherever necessary. They can provide security for:

(a) drivers who need to be seated when operating mobile work equipment, for example the seat on a site dumper;

(b) people who need to be seated while being transported by the mobile work equipment, for example bench seats in mine locomotive manriding carriages; and

(c) people who are involved in on-board work activities which are best carried out in a seated position.

Cabs, operators' stations and work platforms

329 Cabs, operators' stations and work platforms, with suitable side, front and rear barriers or guard rails can prevent people from falling from mobile work equipment when it is travelling. Where provided, they should be properly designed and constructed. They can be fully enclosed or may be open to the environment.

Equipment not specifically designed for carrying people

330 Under exceptional circumstances mobile work equipment may be used to carry people although it is not specifically designed for this purpose, for example trailers used to carry farmworkers during harvest time. Under these circumstances the mobile work equipment must have features to prevent people falling from it and to allow them to stabilise themselves while it is travelling, for example trailers with sides of appropriate height or by providing a secure handhold. People would also need to be able to safely mount and dismount.

Falling object protective structures (FOPS)

331 If people carried on the mobile work equipment are at significant risk of injury from objects falling on them while it is in use, a FOPS should be provided. This may be achieved by a suitably strong safety cab or protective cage which provides adequate protection in the working environment in which the mobile equipment is used.

Restraining systems

332 The need for restraining systems on mobile work equipment is determined by the risks to workers operating and riding on the mobile work equipment and the practicability of fitting and using such restraints. Restraining systems can be full-body seat belts, lap belts or purpose-designed restraining systems. When assessing the need for restraining systems and the nature of seat restraint required, the risk of people being injured through contact with or being flung from the mobile work equipment if it comes to a sudden stop, or moves unexpectedly, should be taken into account. The need for protection against risks for rolling over and overturning (regulations 26 and 27) should also be taken into account when deciding whether restraining systems should be fitted.

Speed adjustment

ACOP
Regulation 25

PUWER 98

Guidance 25

333 If work needs to be carried out during the journey, speeds should be adjusted as necessary.

334 When carrying people, mobile work equipment should be driven within safe speed limits to ensure that the equipment is stable when cornering and on all the surfaces and gradients on which it is allowed to travel. In addition, the speeds at which the mobile machinery travels should be limited to avoid sudden movements which could put people being carried at risk. See guidance on motor vehicles in paragraph 65 and on driver training in paragraph 194.

Guards and barriers

ACOP
Regulation 25

PUWER 98

Guidance 25

335 You should ensure that guards and/or barriers fitted to mobile work equipment, which are designed to prevent contact with wheels and tracks, are suitable and effective.

336 Where there is a foreseeable risk to contact with wheels or tracks when mobile equipment is travelling, adequate separation needs to be provided between people and the wheels and tracks. This can be achieved by positioning cabs, operator stations or work platforms and any suitable barriers, such as robust guard rails or fenders, in positions which prevent the wheels and tracks being reached.

Regulation 26

PUWER 98

Regulation 26

Rolling over of mobile work equipment

(1) Every employer shall ensure that where there is a risk to an employee riding on mobile work equipment from its rolling over, it is minimised by -

(a) stabilising the work equipment;

(b) a structure which ensures that the work equipment does no more than fall on its side;

(c) a structure giving sufficient clearance to anyone being carried if it overturns further than that; or

(d) a device giving comparable protection.

(2) Where there is a risk of anyone being carried by mobile work equipment being crushed by its rolling over, the employer shall ensure that it has a suitable restraining system for him.

(3) This regulation shall not apply to a fork-lift truck having a structure described in sub-paragraph (b) or (c) of paragraph (1).

(4) Compliance with this regulation is not required where -

(a) it would increase the overall risk to safety;

(b) it would not be reasonably practicable to operate the mobile work equipment in consequence; or

(c) in relation to an item of work equipment provided for use in the undertaking or establishment before 5th December 1998 it would not be reasonably practicable.

63

When regulation 26 applies

337　In addition to the more general requirements of regulation 25, regulation 26 covers the measures necessary to protect employees carried on mobile work equipment where there are risks from roll-over while it is travelling, for example a moving dumper truck on a construction site or an agricultural tractor forwarding or manoeuvring on a slope.

338　It covers roll-over in which the mobile work equipment may only roll over onto its side or end (ie through 90 degrees) or turn over completely (ie through 180 degrees or more).

339　It does not apply to the risk of mobile work equipment, such as an excavator or a vehicle with a winch, overturning when operating in a stationary position. This is covered by regulation 20.

Risk assessment

340　To assess the likelihood and potential consequences of roll-over, you will need to take into account the following to determine what safety measures are needed:

(a)　nature of the mobile work equipment and any attachments or accessories fitted to it;

(b)　the effects of any work being carried out on or by the mobile work equipment; and

(c)　the conditions in which it is used.

341　When mobile work equipment is travelling, roll-over may be encouraged by uneven surfaces, variable or slippery ground conditions, excessive gradients, inappropriate speeds, incorrect tyre pressures and sudden changes in direction. It can also occur due to the inertia transmitted to the mobile work equipment by attachments used with it, particularly if those attachments are not securely restrained from movement.

342　When mobile work equipment is under power but is restrained from movement, for example when a forestry tractor is being used to drag fallen trees or logs from one place to another and the tree or log snags, you will need to take account of the inherent stability of the mobile work equipment and the forces it can apply.

343　When carrying out a risk assessment it is important to remember that although drivers should be trained to minimise the risk of roll-over, this is not a substitute for hardware measures to prevent roll-over (for example counterbalance weights) or protective structures (for example roll-over protective structures (ROPS) to minimise the risk of injury in the event of a roll-over) WHERE THEY ARE NECESSARY.

Stabilisation

344　Measures that can be taken to stabilise mobile work equipment (ie measures to reduce the risk of roll-over) include fitting appropriate counterbalance weights or increasing its track width by fitting additional or wider wheels. Also, moveable parts which could otherwise create instability by moving around when the mobile work equipment is travelling, may be locked or lashed in stable positions, particularly where locking features are provided for such purposes, for example locking devices for excavator back hoes.

Structures which prevent rolling over by more than 90 degrees

345   Some types of mobile work equipment will only turn onto their sides if roll-over occurs (ie 90 degree roll-over). For example, the boom of a hydraulic excavator, when positioned in its recommended travelling position, can prevent more than 90 degree roll-over.

Regulation 26(1)(b)

346   If parts of the mobile work equipment prevent it rolling over by more than 90 degrees, the requirements of regulation 26(1) will be met.

Roll-over protective structures (ROPS)

347   You should fit suitable roll-over protective structures to mobile work equipment where necessary to minimise the risks to workers carried, should roll-over occur.

Regulation 26(1)(c)

348   ROPS are normally fitted on mobile work equipment which is at risk from 180 degree or more roll-over. They may be structures, frames or cabs which, in the event of roll-over, prevent the work equipment from crushing the people carried by it. ROPS should be capable of withstanding the forces that they would sustain if the mobile work equipment were to roll over through 180 degrees or more.

Limitations on fitting protective structures

349   A protective structure may not be appropriate where it could increase the overall risk of injury to people operating, driving or riding on mobile work equipment. In these circumstances, where possible, the risks of roll-over should be addressed by other means. An example of where protective structures are not appropriate is when mobile work equipment is required to enter and leave buildings with low roofs and contact could increase the risks to workers.

350   In workplaces such as orchards or a glasshouse, it may not be reasonably practicable to operate mobile work equipment fitted with a ROP.

Regulation 26(4)(c)

351   Before fitting ROPS to older mobile work equipment, which has no anchorage points provided on it (in use before 5 December 1998), an engineering analysis would be necessary. The analysis would need to assess whether it is reasonably practicable to fit adequate anchorage points to the equipment and the structural integrity of any anchorage provided. Some mobile work equipment may not be capable of being fitted with protective structures because mounting points of sufficient strength cannot be provided. This will be true of some equipment in use before 5 December 1998. If the risks associated with the use of the equipment are sufficiently high and it is not reasonably practicable to fit mounting points to allow the fitting of a protective structure, you may need to use other equipment which has, or can have, a protective structure fitted to it.

Restraining systems

352 You should provide restraining systems on mobile work equipment, where appropriate, if they can be fitted to the equipment, to prevent workers carried from being crushed between any part of the work equipment and the ground, should roll-over occur.

Regulation 26(2)

353 Where the operator is at risk of falling out and being crushed by the mobile work equipment or its protective structure in the event of roll-over, you should provide a restraining system (for example, a seat belt) if it can be fitted. This restraining system may also be necessary under the more general requirements of regulation 25 to protect against other risks.

354 If the operator is in a fully enclosed protective structure and unable to fall out of the mobile work equipment, they will not be at risk of being crushed between the mobile work equipment and the ground. However, if the operator or people carried are likely to be injured through contact with the inside of the structure during roll-over, a restraining system may be necessary.

Mounting points for restraining systems

355 Any restraining system needs to be fitted to appropriate anchorage points on the mobile work equipment to ensure its integrity and reliability in use. Substantial structural modification may need to made on some older types of work equipment in use before 5 December 1998 to allow a restraining system to be fitted. Under these circumstances it would only be considered reasonably practicable to fit a restraining system if the risks involved were of a sufficiently high order to justify the necessary modifications. Alternatively, you may need to

use other work equipment which has or can have a restraining system fitted to it.

Tractors

356 If a tractor is fitted with a ROP rather than a cab, a restraining system will be needed.

357 Despite compliance with the Agriculture (Tractor Cabs) Regulations 1974, if the operator or people carried are likely to be injured through contact with the inside of the structure during roll-over, it is likely that you will need to provide a seat restraining system.

Overturning of fork-lift trucks

Every employer shall ensure that a fork-lift truck to which regulation 26(3) refers and which carries an employee is adapted or equipped to reduce to as low as is reasonably practicable the risk to safety from its overturning.

What regulation 27 covers

358 This regulation applies to fork-lift trucks (FLTs) fitted with vertical masts, which effectively protect seated operators from being crushed between the FLT and the ground in the event of roll-over, and other FLTs fitted with a ROPS, for example rough terrain variable reach trucks when they are used with fork-lift attachments. Other types of FLT are covered by regulation 26.

Roll-over protection

359   The mast of a vertical-masted FLT will generally prevent an FLT overturning by more than 90 degrees, provided it has sufficient strength and dimensions for this purpose. A variable reach truck FLT, however, is capable of rolling over 180 degrees or more and would need a ROPS to protect the operator if it is used in circumstances where there is a risk of it rolling over.

Restraining systems

360   **For fork-lift trucks fitted with either a mast or a roll-over protective structure, you should provide restraining systems where appropriate, if such systems can be fitted to the equipment, to prevent workers carried from being crushed between any part of the truck and the ground, should it overturn.**

361   If risk assessment shows that an FLT with a seated ride-on operator can roll over in use and there is a risk of the operator leaving the operating position and being crushed between the FLT and the ground, a restraining system, such as a seat belt, will be required. Restraining systems are also required on any FLT which is fitted with a ROPS, for example a variable reach truck to protect operators from the risks of injury from 180 degrees or more roll-over. To be effective, the restraining system should prevent operators or others carried from falling out or being trapped by the FLT or its protective structure in the event of roll-over.

362   There is a history of accidents on counterbalanced, centre control, high lift trucks that have a sit-down operator. Restraining systems will normally be required on these trucks to protect operators from the risks of roll-over.

Where restraining systems are not required

363   Substantial structural modification may be necessary on some older FLTs provided for use before 5 December 1998 in order to allow seat belts or other types of restraining system to be fitted. Under these circumstances it would only be considered reasonably practicable to fit a restraining system if the risks involved were of a sufficiently high order to justify the necessary modifications. Where seat restraints cannot be fitted, and the risks are sufficiently high, you may need to use another FLT which has a restraining system.

Self-propelled work equipment

Every employer shall ensure that, where self-propelled work equipment may, while in motion, involve risk to the safety of persons -

(a)   *it has facilities for preventing its being started by an unauthorised person;*

(b)   *it has appropriate facilities for minimising the consequences of a collision where there is more than one item of rail-mounted work equipment in motion at the same time;*

(c)   *it has a device for braking and stopping;*

(d)   *where safety constraints so require, emergency facilities operated by readily accessible controls or automatic systems are available for braking and stopping the work equipment in the event of failure of the main facility;*

(e)   where the driver's direct field of vision is inadequate to ensure safety, there are adequate devices for improving his vision so far as is reasonably practicable;

(f)   if provided for use at night or in dark places -

(i)   it is equipped with lighting appropriate to the work to be carried out; and

(ii)   is otherwise sufficiently safe for such use;

(g)   if it, or anything carried or towed by it, constitutes a fire hazard and is liable to endanger employees, it carries appropriate fire-fighting equipment, unless such equipment is kept sufficiently close to it.

Regulation 28(a)

Preventing unauthorised start-up

364   Self-propelled work equipment may be prevented from unauthorised start-up if it has a starter key or device which is issued or made accessible only to authorised people. This means that access to starter keys and starting devices, such as removable dumper starting handles, should be controlled. Vehicles designed primarily for travel on public roads are dealt with in paragraph 316.

Regulation 28(b)

Minimising the consequences of a collision of rail-mounted work equipment

365   If more than one item of rail-mounted work equipment can travel on the same rails at the same time and collision may be foreseen, safety precautions are required to control the risks involved. Where necessary, safe methods of working will need to be followed to reduce the chances of rail-mounted work equipment colliding with each other. Where collision may be foreseen, safety precautions, such as buffers or automatic means of preventing contact, should be provided.

Regulation 28(c)

Devices for stopping and braking

366   All self-propelled mobile work equipment should have brakes to enable it to slow down and stop in a safe distance and park safely. To this end, mobile work equipment should have adequate braking capacity to enable it to be operated safely on the gradients on which it will be used and its parking brakes should be capable of holding it stationary (where appropriate, fully loaded) on the steepest incline that the mobile work equipment may be parked in use.

367   Other relevant product legislation exists which deals with braking systems on vehicles which may be used on the road as well as at work, such as the Road Vehicles (Construction and Use) Regulations and Directive 76/432/EEC dealing with tractor braking. Under normal circumstances, vehicles meeting these requirements would be suitable for use at work.

Regulation 28(d)

Emergency braking and stopping facilities

368   Where there are significant risks associated with failure of the main braking device, a secondary braking system is required. The secondary braking system

may operate automatically through spring applied brakes or through a dual circuit system on the service brakes. It may also be operated through the parking brake system or other controls which are easily accessible to the driver. Self-propelled mobile work equipment which will not stop in a safe distance, for example through transmission drag, if service brake failure or faults occur, are normally fitted with secondary braking systems.

Regulation 28(e)

Driver's field of vision

369   This regulation applies when mobile work equipment is about to move or while it is travelling (including manoeuvring). Under these circumstances, where the driver's direct field of vision is inadequate to ensure safety then visibility aids or other suitable devices should be provided so far as is reasonably practicable. Regulation 17 requires that operators of mobile equipment should be able to see anyone who may be put at risk when any control is operated. Therefore, if direct vision is impaired, then mirrors or more sophisticated visual or sensing facilities may be necessary. Regulation 28(e) requires, so far as is reasonably practicable, mobile work equipment to have adequate devices to improve the driver's field of vision where this is otherwise inadequate. Such devices may include mirrors or closed-circuit television (CCTV) and the provision of these devices can be used to meet the requirements of both regulations.

370   Examples of devices which can aid the driver's vision include:

(a)   plane, angled and curved mirrors;

(b)   Fresnel lenses;

(c)   radar; and

(d)   CCTV systems.

The selection of these devices for use on mobile work equipment is a matter for risk assessment, taking account of the purposes for which the devices are provided and their ability to improve driver visibility.

Regulation 28(f)

Equipping mobile work equipment with lighting for use in the dark

371   In terms of this regulation, 'dark' means any situation where the light levels are not good enough for the driver to operate the self-propelled work equipment safely without risks to themselves or other people in the vicinity.

372   In such situations the equipment needs to be equipped with 'appropriate' lighting. The level of lighting required will depend on the type of equipment being operated, how it is being operated and the area in which it is operating. Factors you will need to consider are the presence of other people and/or obstacles in the vicinity of the equipment and ground conditions which could lead to risk. In situations where there is a significant risk of an accident, the lighting will need to be at a sufficient level to help control this risk.

373   Regulation 28(f) only covers lighting on mobile work equipment. Lighting provided at the workplace for the use of all work equipment is covered by regulation 21.

Regulation 28(g)

The carriage of appropriate fire-fighting appliances

374   Where escape from self-propelled work equipment in the event of a fire could not be achieved easily, you should ensure that fire-fighting appliances are carried on that equipment.

375   This regulation covers the risks to the operators of self-propelled work equipment if the equipment itself or any load handled by it catches fire. If the operators cannot readily escape from the equipment (such as from a tower crane), you will need to provide appropriate equipment for extinguishing the fire. This will depend on the type of equipment and/or any load it is intended to handle but could include appropriate extinguishers and fire blankets.

376   For self-propelled work equipment that is used on the public highways carrying a dangerous load, it may need to carry suitable fire extinguishers under the requirements of the Carriage of Dangerous Goods by Road and Rail (Classification, Packaging and Labelling) Regulations 1994. Further guidance is available.[12]

Remote-controlled self-propelled work equipment

Every employer shall ensure that where remote-controlled self-propelled work equipment involves a risk to safety while in motion-

   (a)   it stops automatically once it leaves its control range; and

   (b)   where the risk is of crushing or impact it incorporates features to guard against such risk unless other appropriate devices are able to do so.

377   For the purposes of regulation 29, 'remote-controlled self-propelled work equipment' is self-propelled work equipment that is operated by controls which have no physical link with it, for example radio control. It should be noted that pendant-controlled mobile work equipment is not covered by regulation 29.

378   As part of your risk assessment you need to consider risks, due to the movement of the equipment, to the person controlling it and also anyone else who may be in the vicinity. You may need to consider alarms or flashing lights so that other people in the area are aware of its movement, or presence, sensing or contact devices which will protect people from the risks associated with the equipment, ie if people may come close to or contact it.

379   When the equipment is switched off you must ensure that every part of the equipment which could present a risk comes to a safe stop. If the equipment is controlled manually, the controls for its operation should be of the hold-to-run type so that any hazardous movements can stop when the controls are released.

380   If the equipment leaves its control range, any part of it which could present a risk should be able to stop and remain in a safe state.

Drive shafts

   (1)   Where the seizure of the drive shaft between mobile work equipment and its accessories or anything towed is likely to involve a risk to safety every employer shall -

(a)   *ensure that the work equipment has a means of preventing such seizure; or*

(b)   *where such seizure cannot be avoided, take every possible measure to avoid an adverse effect on the safety of an employee.*

(2)   *Every employer shall ensure that -*

(a)   *where mobile work equipment has a shaft for the transmission of energy between it and other mobile work equipment; and*

(b)   *the shaft could become soiled or damaged by contact with the ground while uncoupled,*

the work equipment has a system for safeguarding the shaft.

Regulation 30(1)

381   A 'drive shaft' is a device which conveys the power from the mobile work equipment to any work equipment connected to it. In agriculture these devices are known as power take-off shafts.

382   'Seizure' refers to stalling of the drive shaft as a result of the operating mechanism of any accessory or anything connected to it becoming incapable of movement due to blockage or some other reason. Under these circumstances regulation 30 applies if the power output of the mobile work equipment is sufficient to cause damage to the connected work equipment which could lead to risk. Regulation 30 does not apply to the risks associated with trapped energy resulting from stalling of the drive shaft if the power output of the mobile work equipment is insufficient to cause damage which could lead to risk. This situation is covered by regulation 19 which deals with the isolation of work equipment from sources of energy.

383   You should assess the risks associated with seizure of the drive shaft. If seizure could lead to risk, for example the ejection of parts, measures should be taken to protect against such risks. For example, slip clutches on the power input connection of the connected work equipment can protect it from damage and guards fitted in accordance with regulation 12 can protect people from ejection risks in the event of equipment break-up.

384   To prevent damage to power take-off shafts in the event of seizure, it is important to use shafts of adequate length. There should be sufficient overlap between the two halves of the shaft to ensure that it is stable in use, to protect against damage when movements occur in the hitch and to ensure that it has sufficient strength. The shaft needs to be capable of sustaining the full power output of the mobile work equipment, taking account of any slip clutches, shear bolts or similar devices which are provided to limit the torque that the shaft would sustain.

Regulation 30(2)

385   To prevent damage to the drive shaft and its guard when the equipment is not in use, the drive shaft should be supported on a cradle wherever one is provided. If there is no cradle, it should be supported by other means to give equivalent protection against damage. You should not rest the drive shafts on draw bars, nor drop them on the ground, as this could lead to damage.

PUWER 98 - REGULATIONS 31-35

PART IV: POWER PRESSES

Regulations 31 to 35 and related Schedules 2 and 3 refer to power presses and are not included here. They can be found in the power presses ACOP.[2]

PUWER 98 - REGULATIONS 36-39

PART V: MISCELLANEOUS

Regulation 36

Exemption for the armed forces

PUWER 98

Regulation 36

    (1)   The Secretary of State for Defence may, in the interests of national security, by a certificate in writing exempt any of the home forces, any visiting force or any headquarters from any requirement or prohibition imposed by these Regulations and any such exemption may be granted subject to conditions and to a limit of time and may be revoked by the said Secretary of State by a certificate in writing at any time.

(2)   In this regulation -

(a)   "the home forces" has the same meaning as in section 12(1) of the Visiting Forces Act 1952;[(a)]

(b)   "headquarters" has the same meaning as in article 3(2) of the Visiting Forces and International Headquarters (Application of Law) Order 1965;[(b)]

(c)   "visiting force" has the same meaning as it does for the purposes of any provision of Part I of the Visiting Forces Act 1952.

(a) 1952 c.67.
(b) SI 1965/1536 to which there are amendments not relevant to these Regulations.

Regulation 37

Transitional provision

PUWER 98
Regulation 37

The requirements in regulations 25 to 30 shall not apply to work equipment provided for use in the undertaking or establishment before 5th December 1998 until 5th December 2002.

Regulation 38

Repeal of enactment

PUWER 98
Regulation 38

Section 19 of the Offices, Shops and Railway Premises Act 1963[(c)] is repealed.

(c) 1963 c.41

Regulation 39

Revocation of instruments

PUWER 98
Regulation 39

The instruments specified in column 1 of Schedule 4 are revoked to the extent specified in column 3 of that Schedule.

Schedule 1

Instruments which give effect to Community Directives concerning the safety of products

Schedule

Regulation 10

(1) Title	(2) Reference
The Construction Plant and Equipment (Harmonisation of Noise Emission Standards) Regulations 1985	SI 1985/1968, amended by SI 1989/1127
The Construction Plant and Equipment (Harmonisation of Noise Emission Standards) Regulations 1988	SI 1988/361, amended by SI 1992/488, 1995/2357
The Electro-medical Equipment (EEC Requirements) Regulations 1988	SI 1988/1586, amended by SI 1994/3017
The Low Voltage Electrical Equipment (Safety) Regulations 1989	SI 1989/728, amended by SI 1994/3260
The Construction Products Regulations 1991	SI 1991/1620, amended by SI 1994/3051
The Simple Pressure Vessels (Safety) Regulations 1991	SI 1991/2749, amended by SI 1994/3098
The Lawnmowers (Harmonisation of Noise Emission Standards) Regulations 1992	SI 1992/168
The Gas Appliances (Safety) Regulations 1992	SI 1992/711
The Electromagnetic Compatibility Regulations 1992	SI 1992/2372, amended by SI 1994/3080
The Supply of Machinery (Safety) Regulations 1992	SI 1992/3073, amended by SI 1994/2063
The Personal Protective Equipment (EC Directive) Regulations 1992	SI 1992/3139, amended by SI 1993/3074, 1994/2326, 1996/3039
The Active Implantable Medical Devices Regulations 1992	SI 1992/3146, amended by SI 1995/1671
The Medical Devices Regulations 1994	SI 1994/3017
The Electrical Equipment (Safety) Regulations 1994	SI 1994/3260
The Gas Appliances (Safety) Regulations 1995	SI 1995/1629
The Equipment and Protective Systems Intended for Use in Potentially Explosive Atmospheres Regulations 1996	SI 1996/192
The Lifts Regulations 1997	SI 1997/831

1

Schedule 4

Revocation of instruments

Schedule

Regulation 39

(1) Title	*(2)* Reference	*(3)* Extent of revocation
The Operations at Unfenced Machinery (Amended Schedule) Regulations 1946	S.R. & O. 1946/156	The whole Regulations
The Agriculture (Circular Saws) Regulations 1959	SI 1959/427	The whole Regulations
The Prescribed Dangerous Machines Order 1964	SI 1964/971	The whole Order
The Power Presses Regulations 1965	SI 1965/1441	The whole Regulations
The Abrasive Wheels Regulations 1970	SI 1970/535	The whole Regulations
The Power Presses (Amendment) Regulations 1972	SI 1972/1512	The whole Regulations
The Woodworking Machines Regulations 1974	SI 1974/903	The whole Regulations
The Operations at Unfenced Machinery (Amendment) Regulations 1976	SI 1976/955	The whole Regulations
The Factories (Standards of Lighting) (Revocation) Regulations 1978	SI 1978/1126	The whole Regulations
The Offshore Installations (Application of Statutory Instruments) Regulations 1984	SI 1984/419	The whole Regulations
The Offshore Installations (Operational Safety, Health and Welfare and Life-Saving Appliances) (Revocations) Regulations 1989	SI 1989/1672	The whole Regulations
The Provision and Use of Work Equipment Regulations 1992	SI 1992/2932	The whole Regulations
The Construction (Health, Safety and Welfare) Regulations 1996	SI 1996/1592	Regulation 27

4

Schedule 1 of the Reporting of Injuries, Diseases and Dangerous Occurrences Regulations 1995

1   Any fracture, other than to the fingers, thumbs or toes.

2   Any amputation.

3   Dislocation of the shoulder, hip, knee or spine.

4   Loss of sight (whether temporary or permanent).

5   A chemical or hot metal burn to the eye or any penetrating injury to the eye.

6   Any injury resulting from an electric shock or electrical burn (including any electrical burn caused by arcing or arcing products) leading to unconsciousness or requiring resuscitation or admittance to hospital for more than 24 hours.

7   Any other injury:

(a)   leading to hypothermia, heat-induced illness or to unconsciousness;

(b)   requiring resuscitation; or

(c)   requiring admittance to hospital for more than 24 hours.

8   Loss of consciousness caused by asphyxia or by exposure to a harmful substance or biological agent.

9   Either of the following conditions which result from the absorption of any substance by inhalation, ingestion or through the skin:

(a)   acute illness requiring medical treatment; or

(b)   loss of consciousness.

10   Acute illness which requires medical treatment where there is reason to believe that this resulted from exposure to a biological agent or its toxins or infected material.

Further guidance on regulation 11 - Dangerous parts of machinery

Explanation of safeguarding terms, regulation 11(2)

1   GUARDS are physical barriers which prevent access to the danger zone. FIXED GUARDS in regulation 11(2)(b) have no moving parts and are fastened in a constant position relative to the danger zone (see Figure 1). They are kept in place either permanently, by welding for example, or by means of fasteners (screws, nuts, etc) making removal/opening impossible without using tools. If by themselves, or in conjunction with the structure of the equipment, they ENCLOSE the dangerous parts, fixed guards meet the requirements of the first level of the hierarchy. Note that fixed enclosing guards, and other types of guard, can have openings provided that they comply with appropriate safe reach distances (see BS EN 294: 1992).

2   OTHER GUARDS in regulation 11(2)(b) include movable guards which can be opened without the use of tools, and fixed guards that are not fully enclosing. These allow limited access through openings, gates, etc for feeding materials, making adjustments, cleaning, etc (see Figure 2). MOVABLE GUARDS may be power-operated, self-closing, adjustable, etc and are likely to require an interlocking device so that:

(a)   the hazardous machine functions covered by the guard cannot operate until the guard is closed;

(b)   if the guard is opened while hazardous machine functions are operating, a stop instruction is given;

(c)   when the guard is closed, the hazardous machine functions covered by the guard can operate, but the closure of the guard does not by itself initiate their operation.

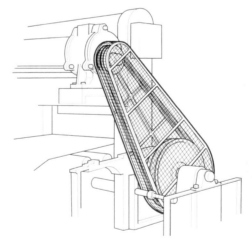

Figure 1 Fixed enclosing guard

Interlocking guards may be fitted with a locking device so that the guard remains closed and locked until any risk of injury from the hazardous machine fuctions has passed. A control guard (interlocking guard with a start function) is a particular type of interlocking guard which should be used only in certain situations where frequent access is required. It should also fulfil specific conditions, in particular, where there is no possibility of an operator or part of their body remaining in the danger zone or between the danger zone and the guard while the guard is closed (see BS EN 953: 1998).

3   PROTECTION DEVICES are devices which do not prevent access to the danger zone but stop the movement of the dangerous part before contact is made. They will normally be used in conjunction with a guard. Typical examples are mechanical trip devices, active opto-electronic devices such as light curtains (see Figure 3), pressure-sensitive mats and two-hand controls.

4   PROTECTION APPLIANCES are used to hold or manipulate in a way which allows operators to control and feed a loose workpiece at a machine while keeping their body clear of the danger zone. They are commonly used in conjunction with manually fed woodworking machines (see Figure 4) and some other machines such as bandsaws for cutting meat where it is not possible to fully guard the cutting tool. These appliances will normally be used in addition to guards.

5   Adequate INFORMATION, INSTRUCTION, TRAINING AND SUPERVISION are always important, even if the hazard is protected by hardware measures, however, they are especially important when the risk cannot be adequately eliminated by the hardware measures in regulation 11(2)(a) to (c). It may be necessary to lay down procedures to define what information, instruction, training and supervision must be given, and to restrict use of the equipment to those who have received such instructions etc.

Selection of measures

6   The guidance outlines how the hierarchy in regulation 11(2) should be applied in selecting safeguarding measures. Within each level of the hierarchy, there may be some choice available. In particular, the second level in the hierarchy allows a choice from among a number of different types of guard or protection device.

7   Regulation 11(2)(b) requires that when it is not practicable to use fixed enclosing guards, either at all or to the extent required for adequate protection, other guards and/or protection devices shall be used as far as practicable. Where, for example, frequent access is required, it may be necessary to choose between an interlocking movable guard or a protection device. The foreseeable probability and severity of injury will influence the choice of measures from among the range of guards and protection devices available. Regulation 11(3)(a) requires that these must be suitable for their purpose. It is likely that some fixed guarding will be required to ensure that access can only be made through the movable opening guard or protection device. The use of movable guards which are interlocked is well established. Protection devices need to be carefully applied, taking into account the particular circumstances and the consequences of their failing to act as required.

8   Fixed distance guards, adjustable guards and other guards which do not completely enclose the dangerous parts should only be used in situations where it is not practicable to use fixed enclosing guards or protection devices which would give a greater level of protection.

Features of guards and protection devices, regulation 11(3)

Regulation 11(3)(a)

9   All guards and protection devices provided must be suitable for their purpose. In deciding what is suitable, employers should first establish the foreseeable risks from the machine and then follow guidance contained in national and international standards (see the reference section), guidance from HSC, HSE and industry associations, normal industrial practice and their own knowledge of the particular circumstances in which the machine is to be used.

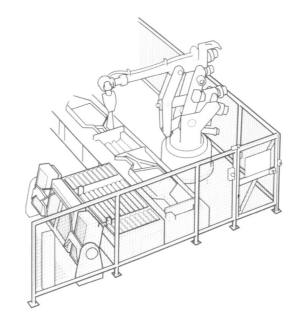

Figure 2 Perimeter fence guard with fixed panels and interlocking access door

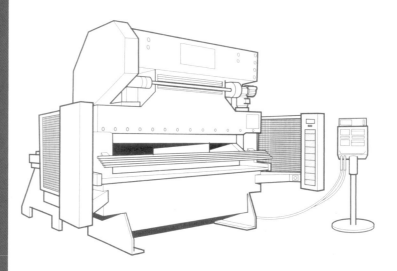

Figure 3 Photoelectric device fitted to a press brake

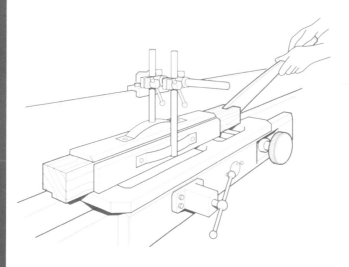

Figure 4 A push stick in use at a woodworking machine

10   A protection device or interlocking system should be designed so that it will only operate as intended. Furthermore, if a component deteriorates or fails, the device or system should as far as possible fail in a safe manner by inhibiting the dangerous action of the machine. The force of this requirement depends on the combination of probability of failure and severity of the injury, should the system fail. If the overall risk is high, there should be adequate provision to counteract the effects of failure. Guidance on appropriate levels of protection is given in the publications referred to in paragraph 9 of this Appendix.

Regulation 11(3)(b)

11   Guards and protection devices must be of good construction, sound material and adequate strength. They must be capable of doing the job they are intended to do. Several factors can be considered:

(a)   material of construction (metal, plastic, laminated glass, etc);

(b)   form of the material (sheet, open mesh, bars, etc);

(c)   method of fixing.

12   Good construction involves design and layout as well as the mechanical nature and quality of the construction. Foreseeable use and misuse should be taken into account.

Regulation 11(3)(c)

13   Guards and protection devices must be maintained in an efficient state, in efficient working order and in good repair. This is an important requirement as many accidents have occurred when guards have not been maintained. It is a particular example of the general requirement under regulation 5 to maintain equipment. Compliance can be achieved by the use of an effective check procedure for guards and protection devices, together with any necessary follow-up action. In the case of protection devices or interlocks, some form of functional check or test is desirable.

14   For inspection and thorough examination of power presses and their guards and protection devices, see the Approved Code of Practice and guidance *Safe use of power presses.*[2]

Regulation 11(3)(d)

15   Guards and protection devices must not themselves lead to any increased risk to health or safety. One effect of this sub-paragraph is to prevent use of inherently hazardous measures for guarding.

16   A second effect is that guards must be constructed so that they are not themselves dangerous parts. If a guard is power operated or assisted, the closing or opening action might create a potentially dangerous trap which needs secondary protection, for example a leading-edge trip bar or pressure-sensitive strip.

17   The main concern is the overall effect on risk. The fact that a guard may itself present a minor risk should not rule out its use if it can protect against the risk of major injury. For example, sweep-away guards or manually-actuated sliding access gates might be able to cause minor injury, but their use in guarding against more serious risks is justified.

Regulation 11(3)(e)

18   Guards and protection devices must be designed and installed so that they can not be easily bypassed or disabled. This refers to accidental or deliberate action that removes the protection offered. By regulation 11(3)(a), guards must be suitable for their purpose, and one consequence of this is that simple mechanical bypassing or disabling should not be possible.

19   Movable panels in guards giving access to dangerous parts or movable guards themselves will often need to be fitted with an interlocking device. This device must be designed and installed so that it is difficult or impossible to bypass or defeat. Guidance on the selection and design of interlocking devices is available from BS EN 1088: 1996 and the sources listed in paragraph 9 of this Appendix.

20   In some cases, bypassing is needed for a particular purpose such as maintenance. The risks arising in such circumstances must be carefully assessed. As far as possible, the risks should be reduced or eliminated by appropriate design of the machinery - see regulation 22.

Regulation 11(3)(f)

21   Guards and protection devices must be situated at a sufficient distance from the danger zone they are protecting. In the case of solid fixed enclosing guards, there is no minimum distance between guard and danger zone, except that required for good engineering design. However, the gap between a fence type guard or protection device and machine should normally be sufficiently small to prevent anybody remaining in it without being detected; alternatively, the space between guard or protection device and machine should be monitored by a suitable presence-sensing device.

22   Where guarding is provided with holes or gaps (for visibility, ventilation or weight reduction, for example), or is not fully enclosing, the holes must be positioned or sized so that it prevents foreseeable access to the danger zone. Published national and international standards (for example, BS EN 294: 1992) give guidance on suitable distances and opening sizes in different circumstances.

23   The positioning of protection devices which enable hazardous machine operation to stop before access can be gained to its danger zone will be affected by both the characteristics of the device itself (response time) and those of the machine to which it is fitted (time needed to stop). In these circumstances the device must be positioned so that it meets published criteria for the performance of such a system. Refer to the relevant standard (BS EN 999: 1998) and guidance (HSG180).[13]

24   Safeguarding is normally attached to the machine, but the regulation does preclude the use of free-standing guards or protection devices. In such cases, the guards or protection devices must be fixed in an appropriate position relative to the machine.

Regulation 11(3)(g)

25   Guards and protection devices must not unduly restrict the view of the operating cycle of the machinery, where such a view is necessary. It is not usually necessary to be able to see all the machine; the part that needs to be seen is normally that which is acting directly on material or a workpiece.

26   Operations for which it is necessary to provide a view include those where the operator controls and feeds a loose workpiece at a machine. Examples

include manually fed woodworking machines and food slicers. Many of these operations involve the use of protection appliances.

27   If the machine process needs to be seen, but cannot be, there is a temptation for the operator to remove or disable guards or interlocks. In such cases, some view of the work may be considered necessary. Examples are a hopper feeding a screw conveyor, milling machines, and power presses.

28   In other cases it may be convenient but not absolutely necessary to see the entire operating cycle. The regulation does not prohibit providing a view in these cases, but does not require it; an example is an industrial tumble drier.

29   Where an operation protected by guards needs to be seen, the guard should be provided with viewing slits or properly constructed panels, perhaps backed up by internal lighting, enabling the operator to see the operation. The arrangements to ensure visibility should not prevent the guarding from carrying out its proper function; but any restriction of view should be the minimum compatible with that. An example of a guard providing necessary vision is viewing slits provided in the top guard of a circular saw.

Regulation 11(3)(h)

30   Guards and protection devices must be constructed or adapted so that they allow operations necessary to fit or replace parts and for maintenance work, restricting access so that it is allowed only to the area where the work is to be carried out and, if possible, without having to dismantle the guard or protection device.

31   This regulation applies to the design of guards or protection devices so as to reduce risks arising from some particular operations. Regulation 22 applies to the design of equipment as a whole so that maintenance and similar operations can be carried out safely; regulation 11 is restricted to machine safeguards.

32   The aim is to design the safeguards so that operations like fitting or changing parts or maintenance can be done with minimal risk. If risk assessment shows this is not already the case, it may be possible to adapt the safeguarding appropriately.

33   Ideally, the machine is designed so that operations can be done in an area without risk, for example by using remote adjustment or maintenance points. If the work has to be done in the enclosed or protected area, the safeguarding should be designed to restrict access just to that part where the work is to be carried out. This may mean using a series of guards.

34   If possible, the guard or protection device should not have to be dismantled. This is because of the possibility that after reassembly, the guard or device may not work to its original performance standard.

Regulation 11(4)

35   Protection appliances also need to be suitable for their application. Factors for consideration come under the same headings as those for guards and protection devices as in regulation 11(3). Many of these are common sense matters. Their design, material, manufacturer and maintenance should all be adequate for the job they do. They should allow the person to use them without having to get too close to the danger zone, and they should not block the view of the workpiece.

81

References

1   *Safe use of lifting equipment. Lifting Operations and Lifting Equipment Regulations 1998. Approved Code of Practice and Guidance on Regulations* L113 HSE Books ISBN 0 7176 1628 2

2   *Safe use of power presses. Provision and Use of Work Equipment Regulations 1998 as applied to power presses. Approved Code of Practice and Guidance on Regulations* L112 HSE Books ISBN 0 7176 1627 4

3   *Safe use of woodworking machinery. Provision and Use of Work Equipment Regulations 1998 as applied to woodworking. Approved Code of Practice and Guidance Regulations* L114 HSE Books ISBN 0 7176 1630 4

4   *5 steps to risk assessment* INDG163(rev) HSE Books 1998 (single copies free; ISBN 0 7176 1565 0 for priced packs)

5   *Managing health and safety: Five steps to success* Leaflet INDG275 HSE Books 1998 (single copy free or priced packs of 10 ISBN 0 7176 2170 7)

6   *Workplace transport safety* HSG136 HSE Books 1995 ISBN 0 7176 0935 9

7   *Safe work in confined spaces* INDG258 HSE Books 1997

8   *Control of substances hazardous to health. The Control of Substances Hazardous to Health Regulations 2002. Approved Code of Practice and guidance* L5 (Fourth edition) HSE Books 2002 ISBN 0 7176 2534 6

9   *A guide to the Health and Safety (Consultation with Employees) Regulations 1996* L95 Guidance on Regulations HSE Books 1995 ISBN 0 7176 1234 1

10 *Buying new machinery* INDG271 HSE Books (single copies free; ISBN 0 7176 1559 6 for priced packs)

11 *Lighting at work* HSG38 HSE Books 1998 ISBN 0 7176 1232 5

12 *Working with ADR: An introduction to the carriage of dangerous goods by road* Leaflet 04DFT01 Department for Transport 2004. Available from DfT Publications, PO Box 236, Wetherby, West Yorkshire LS23 7NB Tel: 0870 1226 236 Fax: 0870 1226 237 e-mail: dft@twoten.press net Website: www.publications.dft.gov.uk

13 *The application of electro-sensitive protective equipment employing light curtains and light beam devices to machinery* HSG180 HSE Books 1998 ISBN 0 7176 1550 2

Further reading

Essentials of health and safety at work HSE Books 1994 ISBN 0 7176 0716 X

Management of health and safety at work. Management of Health and Safety at Work Regulations 1999. Approved Code of Practice L21 HSE Books 2000 ISBN 0 7176 2488 9

Workplace health, safety and welfare. Workplace (Health, Safety and Welfare) Regulations 1992. Approved Code of Practice and Guidance L24 HSE Books 1992 ISBN 0 7176 1413 6

A step by step guide to COSHH assessment HSG97 (Second edition) HSE Books 2004 ISBN 0 7176 2785 3

Occupational exposure limits: Containing the list of maximum exposure limits and occupational exposure standards for use with the Control of Substances Hazardous to Health Regulations 1999 Environmental Hygiene Guidance Note EH40 (revised annually) HSE Books 2002 ISBN 0 7176 2083 2

Occupational exposure limits: Supplement 2003 Environmental Hygiene Guidance Note EH40/2002 HSE Books 2003 ISBN 0 7176 2172 3

Rider-operated lift trucks. Operator training. Approved Code of Practice and guidance L117 HSE Books 1999 ISBN 0 7176 2455 2

Industrial robot safety: Your guide to the safeguarding of industrial robots HSG43 (Second edition) HSE Books 2000 ISBN 0 7176 1310 0

The Supply of Machinery (Safety) Regulations 1992 SI 1992 No 3073 HMSO ISBN 0 11 025719 7

The Supply of Machinery (Safety) (Amendment) Regulations 1994 SI 1994 No 2063 HMSO ISBN 0 11 045063 9

The Electrical Equipment (Safety) Regulations 1994 SI 1994 No 3260 HMSO ISBN 0 11 043917 1

The future availability of the publications listed in this guidance cannot be guaranteed.

Printed and published by the Health and Safety Executive   C150   6/04